THE UNFOLDING DRAMA

THE UNFOLDING DRAMA

Studies in U.S. History
by Herbert Aptheker

Edited by Bettina Aptheker

INTERNATIONAL PUBLISHERS, New York

Copyright © 1978 by International Publishers
All rights reserved
First Edition, 1979
Manufactured in the United States of America

Library of Congress Cataloging in Publication Data

Aptheker, Herbert, 1915-
   The unfolding drama.

   Includes bibliographical references and index.
   I. United States History Addresses, essays,
lectures. I. Aptheker, Bettina. II. Title.
E178.6.A66   973   78-21025
ISBN 0-7178-0560-3
ISBN 0-7178-0501-8 pbk.   79-5767

CONTENTS

The American War is over, but this is far from
being the case with the American Revolution.
On the contrary, nothing but the first act
of the great drama is closed.

BENJAMIN RUSH
at the Constitutional Convention, 1787

FOREWORD

As the United States enters its third century, "futurologists"—that new breed of sociologist obsessed with avowing the survival of capitalism—continue to forecast a remarkably cheerful outlook for the bourgeoisie in the year 2000. Puzzled by the seeming incongruity between this, and the prevailing pessimism about the future of anything in most other professional circles, I scanned the futurological literature. Four striking things emerged.

First, Black people, when they are mentioned (which is not very often) are always discussed in terms of the threat they pose to the new super-industrial society. Alvin Toffler, for example, in his *Future Shock,* warns that "in the new fast-paced, cybernetic society, this minority can, by sabotage, strike or a thousand other means disrupt the entire system."

Black people pose a technical problem for the social engineer of the future. How shall they be contained? Toffler, being of relatively liberal persuasion, suggests "bringing them into the system as full partners, permitting them to participate in social goal setting . . . ." A minority, Toffler maintains, "so laced into the system" is far less likely to be disruptive.

Others, less liberal in their world view, suggest different solutions: preventive detention, psycho-surgery, surveillance via an electronic impulse implanted in the brain. Behavior modification, through the use of electric shock or the more sophisticated drug-induced sensation of asphyxiation, is an increasingly fashionable solution.

The second striking feature of the futurological realm is the disposition of women. Women are discussed in terms of their relationship to men; that is to say, as sexual objects. The primary problem for the (male) futurologist then, is the impact of the technological/biological changes on the future of sexual relations, family structure and women as the bearers of children.

"When babies can be grown in a laboratory jar what happens to the very notion of maternity?" Toffler queries. He continues: "If embryos are for sale, can a corporation buy one? Can it buy ten thousand? Can it resell them? . . . If we buy and sell living embryos are we back to some form of slavery?" Toffler says these are some of the really pressing issues we must resolve.

The third notable feature of the futurological rendition is that by the year 2,000 there will apparently be no more Native American Indian, Chicano, Latino, Puerto Rican or Asian peoples in the United States. At least there is no mention of them in the futurological references surveyed. Presumably, by then, someone will have engineered the final solution to this problem.

The fourth distinctive feature of future society is the disappearance of the working class, and with it the class struggle. This is not really explained; it is simply assumed.

Unable to cope with the enormity of the social chaos created by capitalism these future-focused sociologists have abandoned even the pretense of reform. Instead, they propose the containment and/or extinction of all "problems."

Once having contained or eliminated Black, Chicano, Asian and Native American Indian peoples, women and workers, they can allow their imaginations to run wild. In ecstasy they anticipate their future push-button "James Bond" world of instant comfort, instant food, instant sex and disposable people.

The bourgeoisie creates a futurological spectacular in its own image, a technological wonderland finally stripped of all humanity, all meaning and all purpose. Sensing the end, the bourgeois rulers frantically seek Utopia, and so write their own epitaph.

As futurologists have sought to contain and/or eliminate the "problem" of the poor and the oppressed, so most bourgeois historians have sought to obscure and deny their history. And for very much the same reason. "The present is made up of the past," Herbert Aptheker writes, "and the future is the past and the present dialectically intertwined. Controlling the past," he continues, "is of great consequence in determining the present and shaping the future . . . ." Indeed, the futurological offering is an exact replication of predominant themes in bourgeois historiography.

In denying the history of the poor and the oppressed the bourgeoisie has also denied their humanity. As Dr. Du Bois put it, in describing his experiences as a graduate student at Harvard at the turn of the century: "The history of the world was paraded before [us] . . . Which was the superior race? Manifestly that which had a history, the white race . . . Africa was left without culture and without history."

Rescuing the history of those whose labor created the wealth of society is the responsibility of the revolutionary scholar; and preserving the record of those whose struggles shaped the basic contours of society is the responsibility of the revolutionary movement. "We have the record of kings and gentlemen ad nauseam and in stupid detail," Du Bois wrote in his introduction to Herbert Aptheker's massive *Documentary History of the Negro People in the United States,* "but of the common run of human beings, and particularly of the half or wholly submerged working group, the world has saved all too little of authentic record and tried to forget or ignore even the little saved."

While on the one hand the bourgeoisie appears to assign little importance to the history of the poor and the oppressed, paradoxically (and understandably), it also devotes enormous energy and resources to the systematic distortion of that history. Acknowledging the paucity of literature on Black women, for example, Angela Davis observed that: "We must also contend with the fact that too many of these rare studies [that do focus on Black women] claim as their signal achievement the reinforcement of fictitious cliches and . . . have given credence to grossly distorted categories through which the Black woman continues to be perceived."

Aptheker, in concluding his thought on the dialectical relationship between past, present and future, notes that: "Hitherto, exploitative ruling classes have gone to great pains to control the past—that is, to write and teach so-called history." In doing so they have been able to divert, or blunt the impact of many democratic and revolutionary movements. This has been especially true as regards the history of the struggle against racism.

From the Marxist perspective the really important epistemological question in history is how ordinary people, working people in particular, have survived a brutal and exploitative system; and resisted, struggled and thereby changed the course of human events. History is not primarily a recitation of dates, or a chronicle of events. It is above all else the critical analysis of social movement.

The definitive character of Herbert Aptheker's work stems primarily from his identification with Marxism. Even the kinds of historical questions Aptheker asked himself reflect the anti-elitist and dynamic qualities of the Marxist methodology. Why else focus on the history of Afro-American people? Why write about labor struggles in the South during slavery; or class conflicts in the South in the decade preceding the Civil War; or slave rebellions? These questions occurred to Aptheker because of the Marxist preoccupation with apprehending the process of change, the nature of causality, and the forward motion of history. They also provided him with a wholly original and unique vantage point from which to view the main currents of United States history.

Herbert Aptheker's first published work appeared in his high school newspaper in 1932. It was called "The Dark Side of the South," and contained his impressions of his first trip to the Southern states. He was then sixteen years old. That same year the trial of the Black Communist, Angelo Herndon, took place in Georgia. Herndon was charged with insurrection as a consequence of his activities in the movement of the unemployed. He was convicted and sentenced to twenty years on the Georgia chain gang. The intervention of world public opinion, organized by the Communist Party of the United States, forced Herndon's release before the sentence could be executed. One of Aptheker's earliest memories is of a mobile exhibit, prepared by the Herndon defense committee in New York City, which toured the neighborhood where he lived. The exhibit displayed a cage, with the figure of a Black man chained inside, to dramatize the Herndon case.

By 1938, and for the next several years, Aptheker was again in the South, this time as an educational worker for the Food and Tobacco Workers Union. Working with him was the Black Communist and leader of the Southern Negro Youth Congress, Louis E. Burnham. Aptheker joined the Communist Party in 1939. Shortly thereafter he served as Secretary of the Abolish Peonage Committee. Two months after the United States entered the Second World War Aptheker joined the army, asked to be assigned to Black troops, and fought in the European theater. His outfit took Düsseldorf. He was in Paris on V.E. Day.

Infused through all of Aptheker's scholarship is a definite, even passionate partisanship for the oppressed. Much of this, I think, stems from his experiences in the movement, and in the war; and, from the very special kind of support and encouragement given him by workers in general, and Black workers in particular. For example, while assembling the material for his study of *American Negro Slave Revolts,* Aptheker often had difficulty obtaining the documents he requested from white officials in the Southern archives. During one memorable search it was the Black caretaker who let him into the archives after dark, located the documents in question, and assisted in putting them together.

This collection of Herbert Aptheker's writings is based exclusively on his work in U.S. history. Many of these selections have long been out-of-print, and most have never appeared in book form. The origin of each item is indicated. No substantive changes have been made. A bibliographical comment at the end provides something of an overview of Aptheker's contribution to U.S. historiography. Related books and articles which he has produced are also cited.

It has been an honor and a privilege to select, arrange and edit this collection of Herbert Aptheker's writings. It is hoped that the effort may be worthy of Aptheker as historian. In any event, it is certain that this historical record, as created by Herbert Aptheker, portends a future somewhat more conducive to human values than the grotesque fantasies of the futurologists.

BETTINA APTHEKER

THE UNFOLDING DRAMA

part **I**

WRITING HISTORY

1
FOUNDING THE REPUBLIC

The Revolutionary Character
of the American Revolution

In the United States today there are two apparently contradictory views
of the American Revolution which dominate the news media, the
publishing industry and academia. One, associated with the attitude of
the Daughters of the American Revolution and given sophisticated
reiteration in the writings of Daniel J. Boorstin, among many others,
holds that the unique feature of the American Revolution was that it
was not a revolution, or at most, that it was a conservative revolution.
This concept fills the official pronouncements and spirit of the Bicentennial Commission of the United States Government.

The other view holds that the American Revolution was a perfect one
in conception and execution; that it was the quintessence of human
accomplishment and that its applicability to the present is complete. To
the degree that this view emphasizes the shortcomings of present-day
U.S. society and dominant policy, it possesses progressive elements; but
in its tendency to make the event of the eighteenth century an un-
blemished model for all time, it falsifies history and tends to reinforce
the foundations of the status quo, especially since it ignores the
hegemony in that revolution of the classes possessing the means of
production, which, then, included not only the bourgeoisie but also the

slaveowners. Such a view of the Revolution results not only in down-playing the reality of class differentiation and struggle in the America of the eighteenth century; it also tends to minimize—or even ignore—the realities of chattel slavery and of the genocidal policy pursued toward the Indian peoples and the vile racism that served as the rationalization and prop for both atrocities.

Seeing the Revolution in this uncritical and false manner tends also to support the quite conservative and reactionary view that holds that a revolutionary outlook in the present for an American is on its face un-American and truly alien. This was the characteristic view of such notorious reactionaries, for example, as the late Nicholas Murray Butler, formerly president of Columbia University, who insisted that since—in his opinion—the Revolution of the eighteenth century pro-duced a perfect society or at least a model for a perfect society and even a method for alterations should blemishes appear, one who lived in this paradise and still retained a revolutionary outlook was either a mad-man or an agent of some hostile foreign power!

There also exists in the United States today, especially among ultra-Leftists and other political infants, an utterly cynical view of the American Revolution in which the event as a whole is simply dismissed as farcical or meaningless or hypocritical or demagogic and other such labels reflecting the emptiness of the heads concocting them. The practical result of this view—as in everything else associated with the ultra-Left—is to assist the ruling class in ballyhooing the Revolution and turning its "celebration" into an occasion for selling toothpaste and deodorants.

The Revolution which resulted in the creation of the United States of America was the product of the interplay of three fundamental forces: a) the contradiction in the relationship between colonizing power and colonists; b) the contradictions within the colonies expressive of their class divisions and the fact that whenever these contradictions reached politically explosive phases the power of Britain was exercised in support of the status quo and in opposition to popular forces; and c) the development through several generations of the sense of a distinction between being an "American" and being an Englishman; that is, the forging of a new nation and therefore of a distinct national conscious-ness. One may add that the dialectical interlocking of these forces served to influence and exacerbate each, so that a) and b) helped in the forging of c) and the latter helped accentuate the former, etc.

Those specific aspects of the Revolution which explain why Lenin could refer to it as "one of those great, really liberating, really revolutionary wars of which there have been so few,"[1] include the following:

The American Revolution was the first successful colonial rebellion in modern history and it marked the overcoming in armed struggle by an aroused population of the greatest military and naval power in the world at that time.

It affirmed in achievement and in theory—as in the Declaration of Independence—the right of national self-determination.

It postulated the equality of all men, again notably in the Declaration of Independence. Of course, its authors meant men and not women and meant propertied men and not indentured men, nor enslaved men, nor colored men; but for its time even the limited meaning of its usage was a significant advance over conditions then prevailing in the world. Furthermore, with the sweep of its language, other times and other societies would universalize the concept so that it would indeed include the great idea of the essential equality of humanity—in its needs, dreams, aspirations and capacities.

The Revolution and the instruments of government resulting from it expounded the concept of popular sovereignty. Again, with those who announced this, its meaning was limited to the concept of "people" in the eighteenth century—male, white, propertied. But many among the people, then, too, read this quite differently. Furthermore, the idea of popular sovereignty was something quite new for hitherto sovereignty inhered in the Sovereign and all these words were spelled with capital letters to reflect the great dignity associated with them and the reverence required. In that sense, the very term "popular sovereignty" was a linguistic innovation if not contradiction and its fullest implementation in all areas of life was and remains the basic agenda of history ever since the eighteenth century.

The Revolution was based on the political theory that the purpose of government *ought to be* one which makes possible among its citizenry—note citizenry, not subjects—"life, liberty, and the pursuit of happiness"—the latter phrase a significant alteration from John Locke's affirmation that government should protect "life, liberty and property."[2] It is not that the Fathers of the Revolution were men who rejected the notion that the security of private property was the basic purpose of government; on the contrary, they accepted this as axiomatic. But, nevertheless, it is noteworthy that the Lockean concept was amended and that the amendment makes possible—indeed, invites—broader and more humane purposes of government than those announced by the seventeenth century revolutionist.

The revolutionists insisted that only a government with the purposes just described was a government; without such purposes so-called government degenerated into tyranny and when such degeneration appeared, the revolutionists declared (and were practicing) that it was not only the right but it was the duty of those inhabiting so afflicted a land to make every effort to alter it, to bring it into accordance with proper aims of government and that if such alteration could only be accomplished through revolution, then that, too, became both a right and an obligation.

The revolutionists came to the conclusion that monarchy and inherited nobility were incompatible with popular sovereignty and with purposes of government which envisaged support for the pursuit of happiness as well as contradicting concepts of human equality. Therefore, they instituted republican forms of government in each of the rebelling colonies and in the central government; in doing this they "smashed" the former state and forged a quite new one. Special attention is to be given to the fact that the two central aspects of the Revolution—independence and a republican form of government—were guaranteed by the Constitution whose adoption sealed the Revolution. That is, just as one would be treasonous if he sought the elimination of the independence of the United States of America so also would one be treasonous if he sought to terminate the republican form of government. Both remained significantly threatened for a generation after the Revolution succeeded in battle, and it is characteristic of revolutions that once successful they do not permit any contesting of the essential purposes of the revolution—whether that be independence and a republic, or independence and socialism. The Constitution of the United States in guaranteeing a republican form of government to each of the states simultaneously is affirming that there is no "freedom" to seek to establish a monarchical form.

More extended notice of the "smashing" of existing colonial state forms may be useful. As the revolutionary process unfolded, beginning in the 1760s, there came into being extra-legal and sometimes illegal organizations of Committees of Correspondence, Sons (and Daughters) of Liberty, Sons of Neptune (reflecting the key role of maritime workers in the revolutionary movement in the cities) and other groups called Associators. All these were tools for communication, propaganda, and, above all, organization; they eventuated into a governing form with a new name and content—a congress—and finally into the Continental Congress. The simplicity of these titles was deliberate and reflected the action-directed and popular nature they possessed. Their presiding officer was called simply "president," though some of the Right in the revolutionary movement suggested more resplendent titles like "Your Highness" or even "Your Majesty." Even the place in the then most populous city—Philadelphia—where the Congress was to meet was a matter of debate, with again the conservative wing of the revolutionary movement urging the State House, hitherto used by the royal officials, as a proper locale. But this was rejected at the invitation of the carpenters of the city and with the agreement of the more radical wing of the revolutionary movement. Thus, the Congress met in the carpenters' hall—the latter now capitalized and rendered as Carpenters' Hall, and much of the population of the United States does not realize that that hall was simply the meeting place of the carpenters (and other mechanics and artisans) of the city.

The concept of popular sovereignty was given flesh and blood insofar as the Revolution did represent the will and the power of the vast majority of the population. Precise figures are not available but all the evidence suggests that at least 70 percent of the population was significantly and consciously part of the revolutionary effort. It was the so-called common people who formed the bulk of the pressure groups, who enforced the boycotts, who rid the country of the king's officers, who formed the armed forces of the Revolution and who bested the greatest military and naval power then in the world.

It is the American Revolution that introduces significant guerrilla warfare with the great names of Marion, Sumter and Fox; and, indeed, the war as a whole so far as the revolutionary forces were concerned was fought in guerrilla style as befits a people's war. That is, the armies of Washington and Greene hit and ran and hit and ran again. Those armies often did the "impossible," crossing icy waters as at Trenton and storming mountains as at Stony Point; and they fought in a way the colonists had learned from the Indians—hiding behind trees and boulders, depending upon individual initiative. For generations after the war, the nobility of England referred to the Americans as "tricky" and "unmanly" for they did not fight in the regulation way that the drafted and mercenary armies employed by European royalty had developed.

The British took all the major cities in rebeldom; they were on the coast and no one then could long withstand the British navy. So New York and Philadelphia and Charleston were taken. But once the British troops moved inland they faced not only accumulating logistical problems but also a hostile population which was not backward in manifesting that hostility.

It was in the South that the British had their greatest military successes and took most territory. That was because some 35 percent of the population therein was made up of chattel slaves and these slaves, having been denied freedom by the revolutionists—though this had been repeatedly demanded—acted in their own behalf. In some cases, where freedom for enlistment was forthcoming, they did join the revolutionary army (perhaps as many as 5,000 did this), but, in general, slaves went to where freedom was and a result was that perhaps as many as 100,000 fled plantations in the South from 1775 through 1783. British commanders in the field suggested to London the wisdom of raising the flag of abolition and affirmed that if this were done the Revolution would be over in the South in a month. London rejected the suggestion because many among the richest slaveowners were themselves Tories and also because the British West Indies contained some 750,000 slaves—and once the flag of abolition is raised it is very difficult to confine it.

A somewhat similar situation prevailed with the perhaps 300,000 Indian population in the colonies. That is, they were not able to unite among themselves and, playing upon this fatal disunity, the Americans and the British were able either to win over or to neutralize certain sections of the Indian peoples. The result was that some among those people fought for one side and some for the other—and some abstained altogether. But, in any case, without unity, successful strategy for themselves was not possible and with the end of the Revolution a policy of federal enmity produced catastrophe for the Indian peoples.

In these two cases in particular the severe limitations of a bourgeois-democratic effort—even in the eighteenth century with the bourgeoisie young and, in a historic sense, progressive—are made palpably clear.

The international quality of the Revolution is outstanding. Of course, in the early stages of the movement, beginning in the 1760s, the colonial protest movement was part of the general protest movement in England. Thus, when the colonists demanded, as they did, "the rights of Englishmen," the King rejected this not only because they were colonists and not Englishmen, but also because, as he said, "if I yield to the mob in Boston, how shall I control the mob in London?" Further, among the colonists, the demands came not only from merchants and planters against commercial and trade policies which, of course, favored the English ruling class; demands came also from seamen and workers and servants and even slaves. These, too, had their particular and very pressing grievances: opposition to the quartering of troops in their homes and neighborhoods; opposition to the employment of British troops in the colonies at wages a fraction of those normally paid colonial workers; the impressing of "common" people into the army and navy of the Crown.

Organized opposition from these masses was a fundamental feature of the American Revolution and to yield to such opposition from such a source meant to the Crown and nobility and ruling circles of Britain (and many of their allies in the colonies) simply the end of civilization.

Significant in the outcome of the war was the refusal of the Canadian population to play a counter-revolutionary role; basic, too, was the revolutionary turmoil in Ireland which led the English Crown to dispatch some of its best troops not to Boston but to Dublin. And, of course, the rising European movement to culminate in the French Revolution had already induced volunteers from France, Holland, Poland, Germany, Denmark, Sweden and Hungary to serve the American cause. In addition, power rivalries between France and England, Spain and England, Holland and England made possible the successes of the diplomacy of the American revolutionaries.

The Revolution did, then, break one of the links in the chain of colonialism. It did overcome monarchy and establish a republican form of government based on the concept of popular sovereignty. It eliminated the last vestiges of feudalism, as primogeniture, quitrent, entail. It contributed to the termination of imprisonment for debt and indentured servitude. It provided for the separation of church and state; it enhanced the concept of education; it helped promote some aspects of the rights of women; it led to the manumission of several thousand slaves and to the elimination of chattel slavery in the North and to some forward movement in the outlawry of the international slave trade.

Some contemporaries wanted more; the mass organizations in particular pressed for further advances, especially in terms of assuring widespread popular political power, curbing economic monopolies and advancing educational possibilities. Some women and a few men did point out the glaring failure to think of and treat women as people and the free Black population petitioned repeatedly for an end to slavery as a cancer which would grow with the growth of the republic and if not excised now at its birthing time would one day threaten the nation's existence.

But the hegemony of the eighteenth century Revolution being in the hands of those who owned the means of production, the severe limitations of such classes—even in their "finest" hour—as to the meaning of "democracy" and of "freedom" were clear. This encompassed the racism born with the birth of capitalism as well as the male supremacist outlook and practice strengthened by that capitalism (and slavery). Above all, the propertied classes held to an overall elitism so that Alexander Hamilton was able to warn of "The People, Sir, the People is a great Beast"; and John Adams was wont to use as synonyms, "the rich, the able and the well-born," and John Jay—first Chief Justice of the United States—felt it to be self-understood that, as he said, "those who own the country should govern it." Even Thomas Jefferson, having in mind urban masses, referred to them as the "swinish multitude."

To them and their classes, freedom meant an absence of restraint, and was a political matter entirely and not at all economic. The economic system under which they flourished was "freedom" so far as they were concerned and the problem of successful government was to restrain tyranny (monarchy) on the one hand and "anarchy" or "chaos" on the other, by which they meant real mass, popular rule. Still, then too, in the eighteenth century, it was the participation and strength of the masses that made possible the success of the Revolution and made possible whatever positive achievements it could and did record. Those achievements—and what they portended—were enough so that there was good reason for the British band that accompanied Lord Cornwallis's surrender to Washington at Yorktown in 1781 to play the tune "The World Turned Upside Down." The music from the British band hinted that this surrender was something new, was not the time-honored ceremony of one monarch's hirelings having bested another, but was rather the triumph of revolutionary republicans.

Lenin, while leading a revolution of an infinitely higher form of democracy—a revolution for socialism—could well appeal to the revolutionary traditions here, in his "Letter to American Workers," and remind them that their country was founded by a "really revolutionary war." That which was most advanced in that revolutionary war came from the brains and experiences and blood and sweat of their class brothers, their fellow toilers in the eighteenth century. In our own era, that which is best in the world and in the body politic of the United States lies in the consciousness and organized strength of working men and women of all colors and all nationalities.

Here in the United States the deepest meaning of the Bicentennial of the Revolution is to comprehend that Revolution as a great milepost of the past 200 years of human history along the way to the achievement of colonial and national liberation, the termination of racism and all forms of elitism and the emancipation of the working class. And it is the victorious working class, it is socialism, which, as a "by-product," brings to fruition for the twentieth century the promises in the immortal manifesto of Revolution, which is the birth certificate of the United States of America.

Published in *World Marxist Review,* Vol. 18, No. 7, July 1975, pp. 100-108.

The Declaration of Independence

The legislature of Virginia discovered this year that the business of the state was interfered with excessively because of a large number of official holidays. It was noted that the birthdays of two sons of Virginia were state holidays—those of Thomas Jefferson and Robert E. Lee—and it was agreed that only one should be so honored. Which was to be retained? There was perfunctory debate; the honorable members quickly agreed to drop Jefferson.

The class which seeks to murder freedom at home and wage war abroad, the class whose morality and perspectives are summed up in the word, McCarthyism, is embarrassed by the memory of our Republic's founder, and charmed by the memory of him who, to perpetuate slavery, led a nearly successful effort to overthrow our Republic by force and violence.

This class, ruling a nation whose sovereignty was won in vindicating the right to self-determination, is now the main bulwark of colonialism and seeks, through corruption and fire, to prevent other peoples from consummating their 1776. In this connection, at the moment, American imperialism's effort to crush the liberation movement in Indo-China immediately comes to mind. It is universally acknowledged that there, as Mark Gayn writes (*The Nation,* June 5, 1954), "in any free election Ho Chi Minh would win by a landslide." So beloved is the man and his cause that even an official of the Bao Dai puppet regime confessed to a *New York Times* reporter (May 9, 1954): "Ho Chi Minh is so greatly revered even on this side that we don't dare attack him in our propaganda."

Admitting of only one answer is the question of this revered leader:

> What would the ancestors of present-day America think, men like Franklin or Jefferson, if they saw American bombers being used to hold back a small nation like ours from gaining our independence?[1]

It is a fact that of 275 descendants of those forefathers, asked (by the *N. Y. Post* and the Madison *Capital-Times* back in 1951) to sign their names, as did Franklin and Jefferson, to the opening paragraphs of the Declaration of Independence, not one would do so. They knew the document's freedom-loving character, and they knew that the red-baiters, in seeking to suppress the ideas of Marx and Lenin, also aimed at the ideas of Franklin and Jefferson.

Life magazine, editorializing some time ago on the Declaration of Independence, posed as being distressed at the tendency, among high government officials and policy makers, to play it down. Said *Life* (July 7, 1952):

> There may be a simple explanation for our soft-pedaling of the Declaration in these years of American leadership: for us to advocate it now entails a new and grave political responsibility for the real consequences, and those are hard to foresee.

Mr. Luce's penman was disingenuous. It is not leadership which induces the soft-pedaling; it is the aims of the leadership, conflicting with the aims of the Declaration, which induce the soft-pedaling. It is because, as the same pen wrote in opening the editorial: "Jefferson's picture still vies with Lenin's in 'backward' young countries like

Indonesia. . . ." "Vies?" No; the pictures hang side-by-side for they complement each other—one the incarnation of eighteenth century anti-feudalism and anti-colonialism, the other the incarnation of twentieth century anti-capitalism and anti-imperialism. One is the exemplar of bourgeois democracy; the other, of proletarian democracy. And these are ideologically and historically related—dialectically, not formally—the latter carrying forward and transforming the former, realizing on the basis of the historically higher economic foundation the higher, socialist, level of democracy. Wrote Lenin:

> . . . just as socialism cannot be victorious unless it introduces complete democracy, so the proletariat will be unable to prepare for victory over the bourgeoisie unless it wages a many-sided, consistent and revolutionary struggle for democracy.[2]

As the imperialists would prevent new declarations of independence by suppressing present-day liberation efforts, so increasingly their historians would emasculate our Declaration of Independence by denying—somewhat retroactively—the existence of the American Revolution.

This is a theme, for example, of Professor Russell Kirk's widely heralded *The Conservative Mind* (Chicago, 1953) and it is expressed at greater length in Professor Daniel J. Boorstin's *The Genius of American Politics* (Univ. of Chicago Press, 1953). The latter finds "the most obvious peculiarity of our Revolution" to have been that "it was hardly a revolution at all." The events mistakenly thought of by George Washington and George III as a revolution were really only a "conservative colonial rebellion." Actually, it was "Parliament that had been revolutionary, by exercising a power for which there was no warrant in English constitutional precedent." The colonists "were fighting not so much to establish new rights as to preserve old ones." No one, then, need be surprised to learn that Professor Boorstin finds the Declaration of Independence to have had a "conservative character."

In the course of our analysis we shall deal with these interesting views.

* * *

What is the meaning of the Declaration of Independence? What are its lessons for today?

The Declaration of Independence expressed the soul of that Revolution and was itself a mighty weapon for its consummation. There are three main streams whose convergence produced that revolution. They sparkle through the lines of Jefferson's "passionate chant of human freedom."

These three streams—interrelated and interpenetrating—are: First, the development of a new nationality, the American, as the result of the colonists' far-flung separation from the imperial power, their life in a new land with different climate, fauna, flora, their representing a new people derived from the blending of a score of peoples, their developing their own history, their own economy, their own common language, the beginnings of their own cultural expressions and their own mode of responding to their environment—their own psychology.

Second, with the planting of the colonies were planted the seeds of the Revolution, for the interests of the rulers of the colonizing power and of the colonists were contradictory and antagonistic. The relationship was that of exploiter and exploited, of dominant and subordinate. There remained only the necessity for the growth in the numbers and strength of the subordinate, the repressed, and the development of a revolutionary consciousness, for the subordination and repression to become more and more onerous and more and more intolerable.

This manifested itself especially in the development of a colonial bourgeoisie—becoming ever more articulate, organized and politically mature—which found increasingly insufferable and therefore unjust the British ruling class's insistence on crippling their development, hampering their trade, taxing their industry, and keeping them from controlling their own immediate market, not to speak of expanding that market or moving out into other areas of trade and profit. This bourgeoisie, young and vigorous, still having before it a century of growth and creativity, had requirements and developed a program consonant with resistance to tyranny, and with the needs of the developing nation. Therefore it could and did offer leadership in the struggle to realize that nation's independence.

Third, the colonies were class societies and, hence, *within* them, class struggle was characteristic. There was, then, not only the trans-Atlantic conflict but also the internal conflict: artisan, mechanic, worker against merchant and boss; slave against slaveowner; yeoman against large planter; debtor farmers against wealthy landowners and creditors. These class struggles permeate all of colonial history and always—from Bacon's Rebellion in Virginia in 1676 to the Massachusetts Land War led by Samuel Adams's father in the 1740s—the forces of the king were arrayed on the side of "law and order" (i.e., exploitation and plunder) and served as bulwarks against the urgent demands of the colonial masses. In this sense the civil-war aspect of the Revolution—the struggle against the homegrown Tories—represented a continuation and a development of earlier internal colonial struggles, just as the trans-Atlantic aspect of the Revolution—the struggle against the king and Lord North—represented a continuation and a development of earlier, external colonial struggles. And just as before the Revolution these struggles had been related, so during the Revolution they were related—indeed, merged.

In this sense, too, one finds not only Patriot and Tory divided, but the revolutionary coalition itself divided. Within that coalition there was a Left, Center and Right, and basic to their differences was exactly the question of independence, of breaking completely from British domination. In the eyes of the Right of the revolutionary coalition such a break meant the loss of a great bulwark of conservatism, of mass exploitation; an impeder of all leveling and democratic aspirations. Hence, there was found resistance and opposition to independence; while, for the contrary reasons, among the Left—speaking as this Left did for the vast majority of the American masses—the urge was for independence. Our history thus demonstrates that from the beginning, from the days of the Revolution, the most devoted patriotism has come from the Left, for it was this Left which was most influential in raising the demand for and in achieving American independence.

Gouverneur Morris of New York put the matter succinctly in a letter of May 20, 1774:

I see, and I see it with fear and trembling, that if the disputes with Britain continue, we shall be under the worst of all possible dominions. We shall be under the domination of a riotous mob [read: the People]. It is to the interest of all men, therefore, to seek for reunion with the parent state.[3]

Morris, in seeking reunion was not, however, seeking subordination, which was the end and the policy of the British government, as it was the purpose of colonization. The same year, surely unbeknown to Morris, the king was writing to his prime minister: "The New England governments are in a state of rebellion. Blows must decide whether they are to be subject to this country or independent."[4]

The king sees no middle way; exploitation is exploitation, and subjection is just that. Reunion on those terms, yes; anything else is rebellion, not reunion. It is this fact and the king's acting on that fact, which defeats the Morris policy, which makes independence indispensable to the American cause and which holds to that cause the revolutionary coalition.

The colonizing power inhibiting the colonial bourgeoisie and oppressing the colonial masses faces the broadest kind of revolutionary movement. For this bourgeoisie, young and progressive, subordinate and oppressed, leads in the effort to throw off the *common* oppressor and gives voice to ideas and to demands not only special to themselves but also meaningful to all components of the revolutionary coalition. Thus the three streams converge, and, under the hegemony of the bourgeoisie, crystallize in revolutionary resistance to imperial domination.

This is the meaning of the colonists' repeated demands for the "rights of Englishmen," for the removal of the "new shackles" as Jefferson put it. Explaining the colonists' position, in a letter written in 1786, Jefferson said their demand amounted to this:

> Place us in the condition we were when the King came to the throne, let us rest so, and we will be satisfied. This was the ground on which all the states soon found themselves rallied, and that there was no other which could be defended.[5]

In this sense there is some truth in Professor Boorstin's remark, already cited, that the colonists "were fighting not so much to establish new rights as to preserve old ones." But preserving old rights under new conditions may itself be "subversive," the more so as the preservation of old rights under new conditions requires the creation of new rights.

How patently wrong, then, is Professor Boorstin when he refers to the British government's exercise of "power for which there was no warrant in English constitutional precedent," as "revolutionary." It was the opposite; it was counter-revolutionary. It was another example of a ruling class grossly violating its own constitutional precedents when those precedents impede the achievement of reactionary ends.

Thus, here, the colonists fight for the "rights of Englishmen," for "no taxation without representation;" and nothing could be a broader demand or one more embarrassing for the Tory propagandists. What, are we not Englishmen? And are we not, then, entitled to the rights of Englishmen and the protection of the splendid English Constitution?

No, this demand is treason, and you are not to have such rights and it is not for this the empire exists; it is to enrich the rulers of Britain, not to equalize the condition of his Majesty's subjects. "If their Treason be suffered to take root," read the King's Speech to the House of Peers, Oct. 31, 1776, "much mischief must grow from it, to the safety of my loyal colonies, to the commerce of my Kingdoms, and indeed to the present System of all Europe."[6]

And the king's chief justice, Lord Mansfield, pointed out, further, that these "rights of Englishmen" claimed by these upstart Americans, this "no taxation without representation," might revolutionize British society itself, for there were millions of Englishmen without such rights, who were taxed but not themselves represented. The demand cut not only at the heart of the colonial system but also at the heart of the home oligarchy which fed on and maintained that system. Shall the king take his law from the rabble of Boston and, if so, how restrain the rabble of London?[7]

The fact is that to obtain "the rights of Englishmen" the colonists had to cease being Englishmen. Moreover, fighting to secure those rights under the new conditions required fashioning new rights altogether: sever church and state; eliminate punishment for "heretical" opinions; provide for full religious freedom; undo the aristocratic system of education; eliminate entail, primogeniture, and quitrent as feudal anachronisms and favorable devices for the building up of a landholding oligarchy; confiscate the king's estates and forests (and those of his Tory adherents); remove all fetters and restrictions on commerce and industry; smash the king's colonial governmental structure and replace it with revolutionary organs; advance the movement against slavery; repudiate His Majesty's divine authority; derive sovereignty from the people's will and, overall, establish, therefore, a *res publica,* a republic.

Such was the "conservative" American Revolution, helping to uproot, as King George III saw, if modern American bourgeois scholars will not, "the present system of all Europe."

Yet, observe, it is the king who hurls down the gauntlet. The colonists confess and possess no disloyalty to their monarch, as they understand him and their position with respect to him. In requesting the rights of Englishmen, they act with the greatest respect, with full legality, and with due deference. They threaten no violence. They see justice on their side and appear to assume that the king and his ministers will see it, too. They are slow to become disillusioned; they are loath to believe the worst:—the British government will not redress their grievances, will not remove the yoke, will not place all subjects of the Crown upon an equal status. No, the British government will add to the grievances, tighten the yoke, reduce the Americans to subordination. As we have seen, the king has told his prime minister, already in 1774, that "blows must decide whether they [the colonists] are to be subject to this country or independent." Blows in reply to peaceable and respectful petitions follow and those blows help cast the die for independence. It is the British government, the forces of repression and reaction, which first resort to a policy of force and violence. That government, through its navy and its army, seeks forcibly to reduce the Americans to subordination and they, then and only then, resort to arms to defend themselves against this force and violence.

And even yet they do not move for independence. The British government outlaws them, blockades their ports, condemns their ships to instant seizure, promises death to their leaders, burns their towns— first all these things are done before history moves from Lexington in April 1775 to the Declaration of Independence in July 1776. Truly, as the Declaration says, "all experience hath shown that mankind are more disposed to suffer, while evils are sufferable" and that governments are not "changed for light and transient causes." No, indeed, wrote Lenin, in the cited *Letter to American Workers,* "we know that revolutions are made neither to order nor by agreement." Yes, revolutionists from Jefferson to Lenin have known well the idiocy of that police-made fantasy—a conspiratorially-concocted, minority-maneuvered "revolution."

*   *   *

Americans declare their independence and stake their lives and sacred honors behind the Declaration, but in the larger and truer sense, the peoples of the world stood behind the Declaration as they have been and continue to be influenced and inspired by it. What are the international ramifications of our great Declaration?

First, the document itself is written because, as its first paragraph says, "a decent respect to the opinions of mankind requires" that this be done. If the people's will is to be supreme, then their good will is omnipotent. So, the Declaration is a broadside to humanity appealing for their support.

Now the Congress (that new-fangled, starkly simple word that terrified the monarchs) which adopted this Declaration had all along been sensitive to world public opinion. One of the first acts of the Continental Congress had been to appoint a Committee on Foreign Affairs, whose main task was to send agents everywhere explaining the justice of the American cause. (This committee is the direct ancestor of the Department of State, an embarrassingly seditious background for Mr. Dulles's bailiwick!) And these agents had had notable success in Canada, in the West Indies, in Ireland, in Europe, and in England itself. Indeed the British Navy was hard put to keep Jamaica, Bermuda, Barbados and the Bahamas from joining the Thirteen, and the cream of the British army was needed during the American Revolution to maintain benign domination in Ireland, while in England itself there were repeated mass demonstrations on behalf of the Americans—and British freedom. (By 1783, Britain, in the Renunciation Act, admitted the claim of the Irish people to be bound only by their own courts and laws.)

In France, as is well known, popular support for the American cause merged nicely with the French king's joy at the tribulations of his English enemy. And it is French willingness actively to support the colonial cause—if that cause encompassed independence, i.e., separation from England—which in turn helped induce congressional approval of independence.

Without international support the Revolution would not have succeeded—certainly not when it did—and those signing the Declaration of Independence might well have signed themselves onto the gallows rather than into immortality. It is only fitting then that this Revolution had colossal impact, in its success, upon the world, and the men from a dozen countries who participated in it—from Haitians to Hessians, from Poles to Frenchmen—helped carry with them the seeds of liberty, equality and the pursuit of happiness. International solidarity is basic to the conduct, success and impact of our Revolution.

Internationalism is central also to the origins of the Declaration's ideas. The 33-year-old Virginian, creating his exquisite and electric sentences (in a room rented from a bricklayer whose father had come from Germany) was distilling and shaping humanist and libertarian arguments from ancient Greece and Rome; from the Irish revolutionist, Charles Lucas; from the Italian economist, Beccaria; from the Swiss philosopher, Vattel, and his compatriot, Burlamaqui; from the German jurist, Pufendorf; from the Frenchmen, Montesquieu, Voltaire, and Diderot; from the Englishmen, Milton, Sidney, Harrington, Locke, and Priestley; and from Americans, too, like Jonathan Mayhew and John Wise. He was, indeed, moved and shaped, by the whole magnificent Age of Reason with its titans who struggled against dogma and authoritarianism—Bacon, Vesalius, Copernicus, Spinoza ... And all of these were products, as they were voices, of the central fact in human history—the struggle against oppression and the dynamic, ever-advancing nature of that struggle. The international sources of the Declaration in no way contradict the national essence of that Declaration. It remains American or, better, therefore, it is American.

With the struggle for the right of self-determination central to the founding of our nation, and with international solidarity fundamental to the achievement of our independence, how violative of these splendid traditions are the present policies of the American ruling class! How incongruous it is to have the government of the United States as the main bulwark of present-day colonialism and national suppression; to have that government as the center of the war danger, seeking to destroy the independence of the peoples of Indo-China, of Korea, of Guatemala—and of all countries that have taken the path to socialism! The ruling class pursuing such policies, besmirches the noble heritage of our country, and threatens its best interests, as it threatens the very lives of all of us. The whole tradition of our Revolution and the whole spirit of our Declaration of Independence cry out against this and call for sympathy and encouragement for all liberation efforts and a policy of peace and friendship with all peoples everywhere.

The three main streams of the American Revolution are merged within its finest expression, the Declaration of Independence. That declaration is expressive of the fact of a new nationality—the American—and of its right to determine its own fate. Thus, when General St. Clair read the Declaration to his troops, on July 28, 1776, he reported that they "manifested their joy with three cheers" and he added:

> It was remarkably pleasing to see the spirits of the soldiers so raised after all their calamities; the language of every man's countenance was: *Now we are a people: we have a name among the States of the world.*[8]

The inter-Atlantic aspect of the Revolution and the internal, civil war character of it appear throughout the "facts submitted to a candid world" which make up the major portion of the Declaration's text. And the development of an equalitarian, democratic public opinion, with powerful organizations mobilizing that opinion, also finds expression in those "facts." But they find particular expression in the great second paragraph of that declaration wherein "self-evident truths" are stated, the true purpose of government affirmed and the right of revolution asserted.

The political theory of the Declaration is intensely democratic and profoundly revolutionary. As Copernicus's discarding the medieval concept of the qualitative inferiority of the earth's movements as compared with those of heavenly bodies helped revolutionize astronomy, so Jefferson's Declaration revolutionized political science by discarding the medieval—feudal—concept of the qualitative inferiority of earthly life as compared with eternal heavenly bliss. This life on earth, Jefferson held, was not supposed to be a vale of tears and suffering. The meaning of life was not unending pain to be endured meekly in order to get into heaven; and man's pain was not his cross because of original sin—because man was evil. And governments were not the secular arm of the Lord, as priests were not his ecclesiastical arms.

No; this entire elaborate machine for the justification and perpetuity of the rigidly hierarchical, non-dynamic, severely burdensome feudal order is denied. Men are good, not evil; men are capable of governing themselves well; governments are man-made; the purpose of life is its ennoblement here on earth. The "freedom and happiness of man," Jefferson wrote to Kosciusko in 1810, are the objects of political organization and indeed "the end of all science, of all human endeavor."[9]

Hierarchy is, then, rejected and with it aristocracy and monarchy and the divine right of ruler or rulers. Equality of man replaces it and therefore sovereignty lies with these equals, and it is their will which is divine, if anything is; at any rate it is their will which will be decisive where government seeks their welfare. And this is dynamic, not static. The idea of progress permeates the whole argument, for with man good, with government well provided, surely then, as Jefferson said, his "mind is perfectible to a degree of which we cannot form any conception," and they speak falsely who insist "that it is not probable that anything better will be discovered than what was known to our fathers."[10]

Hence, too, the right of revolution. For given the above, and the most advanced democratic idea of the time that governments must rest on the consent of the governed, it is clear that where governments oppress, where they do not serve to further happiness, where they stifle and are

engines of exploitation, they are unjust; they have then become tyrannical, and acquiescence in tyranny is treason to man. Thus, Jefferson
taught, the right of revolution is axiomatic where the will of the people
is supreme.

We come, then, to the people's "unalienable rights," to that magnificent phrase, crashing through the corridors of history, "arousing men
to burst the chains,"[11] as Jefferson himself said—"Life, Liberty and the
pursuit of Happiness." And, as we have suggested, it is that "pursuit of
happiness" as man's right, as the just end of government which is the
heart of the revolutionary enunciation and one which, by its magnificent, timeless generalization makes the document meaningful and
stirring for all time.

That Jefferson chose this expression, rather than the usual Whig,
bourgeois-revolutionary one of "Life, Liberty and Property" was deliberate and reflects the advanced position of Jefferson personally and of
the revolutionary coalition which adopted it. True it is, as Ralph B.
Perry has stated, that:

> Property as an inalienable right is not to be identified with any particular
> institution of property, such as the private ownership of capital, or the
> unlimited accumulation of wealth, or the right of inheritance, or the law of
> contract.[12]

True it is, too, that Jefferson conceived of liberty, in the sense of
freedom of speech and press and person, and of the pursuit of happiness, as more elemental, more profound than property rights and this
explains the phrase he chose. It is true, too, that Jefferson—while, of
course, being historically limited, and in no way favoring, or conceiving
of socialism, but on the contrary assuming private ownership of means
of production—was very sensitive to the concentration of property-
holding and felt it to be the central threat to democratic rights. He saw
"enormous inequality" of property ownership—especially in land—as
the cause of "so much misery to the bulk of mankind" that he insisted,
"legislators cannot invent too many devices for subdividing property."[13]

Yet, Jefferson, representative of the rising bourgeoisie, cannot coun-
tenance or see, and the Declaration of Independence does not
enunciate, of course, the class concept of the state. In this sense it is
philosophically idealist, limited—bourgeois. It sees man as such; not
men in class society and the state as the political superstructure and the
instrument of class domination in the given society.

No, the revolutionary bourgeoisie sees the state, which it is capturing and remolding, as an object in itself, standing above classes. And while its insistence that men create it for their purposes is a qualitative leap beyond the feudal concept, there is still an even greater distance from the bourgeois concept to the scientific, Marxist-Leninist, concept of the state.

This supra-class view limits, too, the Declaration's theory of equality, for while this is revolutionary vis-a-vis feudal hierarchical notions, it is largely illusory in terms of the material base of bourgeois society, in terms of property and class relationship, in terms of power, all of which considerations are vital to a scientific, real understanding of equality.

This particular limitation—a limitation of the bourgeoisie even at its finest moment—is strongly illustrated by the fact that while the Declaration spoke of equality and liberty and the pursuit of happiness, 600,000 American slaves were held to labor under the lash. And, as is well known, a passage in Jefferson's original draft of the Declaration, excoriating the king for encouraging that abomination, the slave trade, was cut out because of the objections of Southern slaveowners and Northern slave-traders. This central failing of the Declaration—and of the American Revolution—reflects the organic connection between the rise of capitalism and the enslavement of the Negro people, as it does the system of capitalism and the ideology and practice of racism. For it is most certainly the presence of racism which helps account for the revolutionists going into battle with the slogan "Liberty or Death" on their banners and over half a million slaves on their fields. That which Engels wrote of the Constitution is pertinent to the Declaration: "It is significant of the specifically bourgeois character of these human rights that the American Constitution, the first to recognize the rights of man, in the same breath confirmed the slavery of the colored races in America. . . ."[14]

It is further to be noted, as also reflective of the bourgeois limitations of the movement inspiring the Declaration, that when it said "All men are created equal" it did not mean all men and women, and had this been offered for ratification the document would not have been signed. (Abigail Adams wrote to her husband, John—one of the committee of five entrusted with drafting the Declaration: "I cannot say, that I think you are very generous to the ladies; for, whilst you are proclaiming peace and good-will to men, emancipating all nations, you insist upon retaining an absolute power over wives.")

The achievement of full equality and complete liberty is the task of the working class and its allies; it will represent the realization of freedom—not partial, not potential, but full and actual. But this achievement comes as the culmination of the long and painful and magnificent human record of resistance to oppression and the seeking of liberation.

In this great record, a place of honor is held by the American Declaration of Independence. Butt of cynics, yet scourge of tyrants, that Declaration, written in blood, will live so long as humanity survives.

This birth certificate of our Republic stands in absolute opposition to that travesty upon Americanism which usurps its name, that American brand of fascism—McCarthyism. McCarthyism's contempt for man, its hatred of culture and science, its irrationalism, its cruelty and anti-humanism, its chauvinism, its jingoism, its assault upon elemental democratic rights, all these features of the abomination are directly and exactly contrary to the whole spirit and content of the great Declaration of Independence. In this sense, McCarthyism is profoundly un-American.

The Declaration stands today, as Lincoln said in 1859—when a rabid slave-owning class jeered at it as pernicious and false—as "a rebuke and a stumbling-block to the very harbingers of reappearing tyranny and oppression." Jefferson spoke truly when he said "that the mass of mankind has not been born with saddles on their backs, nor a favored few booted and spurred." Today his admonition arms us: "To preserve freedom of the human mind then, and freedom of the press, every spirit should be ready to devote itself to martyrdom."

We Communists will defend the Declaration of Independence even unto the limits set by Thomas Jefferson, and we will continue to call upon the working class and the people as a whole, to rally for this defense. We are confident that such dedication, helping to arouse the American people to safeguard their most beloved vital document, threatened as it is today by an imperialist ruling class bent on destroying it, will secure our Bill of Rights and make possible further advances in the struggle for democracy, peace, and freedom.

Our Party, standing in the front ranks of fighters against fascism and war, is, as its Draft Program declares, "the inheritor and continuer of the best in American democratic, radical and labor thought and traditions." It is this which "is the source of its deep and abiding patriotism." It is this, too, which moves our Party "to proclaim our fraternity with all peoples who have pioneered the new frontiers of human history toward Socialism, with all peoples struggling to achieve their independence and national development."

In this patriotism and internationalism our Party draws inspiration from, and pays its best tribute to, the American Declaration of Independence.

Published in *Political Affairs, XXXIII, July 1954, pp. 10-22.*

2
PRELUDE TO CIVIL WAR

The Labor Movement in the South During Slavery

The South of slavery times, though conventionally pictured as a placid and untroubled area, actually was marked by intense and multiple social antagonisms. The antagonism between slaves and slaveowners, of course, was basic, but there were several others of great consequence. Among these were the antagonisms between debtors and creditors; landless and landed; artisans, mechanics and industrial workers on the one hand and the owners of ships, railroads, mines, and factories, on the other.

Some work has been done describing and analyzing the raging conflict between slaves and slaveowners, and between non-slaveholding whites (especially rural) and the slaveowners.[1] But very little has been written concerning working-class activity in the South during the existence of slavery.

Long ago, Marx pointed out that, "In the United States of North America, every independent movement of the workers was paralyzed so long as slavery disfigured a part of the Republic."[2] And while slavery would inhibit working-class organization everywhere in the United States, including those areas where the abomination did not exist, it would have a particularly retarding effect in the South, dominated as that section was by slavery.

Nor is it to be believed that the slaveowners were unaware of this "advantage" of their system. On the contrary, the correspondent for the *London Times* in the South during the Civil War was given to under-stand that, "The real foundation of slavery in the Southern States lies in the power of obtaining labor at will at a rate which cannot be controlled by any combination of laborers."[3] While wage figures for the South prior to the Civil War are difficult to find and are widely scattered and fragmentary, all the evidence points to the existence of a considerable wage differential, North and South, with rates of pay "lowest in the South," as a government publication put it.[4]

Yet, the fact remains that where capitalism is, there is a working class, and where there is a working class there is organization. Even in the slave South, with a plantation economy characteristic, with one-third of its entire population held as chattel slaves, and with urbanization and industrialization severely retarded—even there a working class ap-peared, and with it came trade-union organizations, strikes, and politi-cal activity.

Fundamentally because of the enslavement of the Negro masses (there were four million slaves in the South in 1860), and all that went with this enslavement, real development of industry was severely impeded. As a result, the growth of a working class was slow, and its organization on the whole rudimentary. Still, some industrial develop-ment did occur in the slave South, a working class did appear and, consequently, the struggle between capitalists and workers is a part of the history of that slave South. That struggle, consequential in its day, and harbinger of a decisive component of post-Civil War Southern history, deserves the historian's careful attention.

With rare exceptions, however, historians of the slave South have ignored or have slandered working-class activities. The "standard" work in which one would expect, logically—in terms of the title's promise—to find material on the Southern labor movement in the era of slavery is *Life and Labor in the Old South,* by the late Professor Ulrich B. Phillips, first published in 1929. In this work, however, there is nothing on a labor movement, or trade unions. In other works, outright anti-working class prejudices recur, sometimes expressed in almost unbelievably crude language. For example, Professor F. Garvin Davenport's *Ante-Bellum Kentucky: A Social History, 1800-1860* (published in 1943) exhausts the subject of labor in these two sentences:

Several towns, notably Lexington and Louisville, possessed numerous industries which tended to alleviate the unemployment situation but at the same time attracted many undesirable laborers, including free blacks, who became moral and social problems. Nevertheless, the gains from industry were considered of great importance by the contemporary civic leaders and sometimes morally irresponsible laborers were accepted by the entrepreneurs as a necessary evil.(pp.23-24)

Again, Professor E. Merton Coulter, in his *The Confederate States of America, 1861-65* (published in 1950), writes: "Labor organizations and strikes were 'Yankee innovations' and 'abominations' and were practically unknown to the South. . . ." (p. 236)

Other works, not the products of Bourbon pens, normally reflect no improvement in this regard. Thus, the ten-volume *Documentary History of American Industrial Society* (1910), edited by John R. Commons and associates, contains very few and very brief references to Southern labor activity. The first two volumes of *The History of Labor in the United States,* also by Commons and associates (1918), covers the period from the colonial era to 1896, but this was based almost entirely upon Northern and Western sources.

A government publication, *Strikes in the United States,* by Florence Peterson (1938) devotes a chapter to the "Early History of Strikes," but the South, except for reference to Baltimore, is not mentioned. The same omission characterizes Selig Perlman's *A History of Trade Unionism in the United States* (1922); Norman J. Ware's *The Labor Movement in the United States, 1860-1895* (1929); and Foster R. Dulles's *Labor in America* (1949).

Philip S. Foner, in his *History of the Labor Movement in the United States* (Vol. I, 1947), brings forth significant material, especially on the relation of the labor movement in the South to slavery. However, there is still a paucity of work in this area.

In the pages that follow, an attempt is made to record something of the history of the labor movement in the South prior to the abolition of slavery. It is hoped that the effort will not be altogether unworthy of its subject, and that it may serve to stimulate further study of this neglected field.

It is necessary first to dispel the illusion that the South of slavery times was an area containing nothing but plantations and farms, an area devoid of cities and of industry. It is, of course, true that the nation as a whole up to the Civil War was predominantly rural—only 20 percent of the population in the United States lived in cities in 1860. And it is also true that the South was very much behind the North (especially after 1840) in the development of industry and marine and land transportation, but it is equally true that the South was far from having no such developments.

In 1860 there were over 110,000 workers employed in 20,000 manufacturing establishments in the South—about 10 percent of the national total. The factories represented a capital investment of $96 million, which may be compared with the quarter of a billion invested in manufacturing establishments at that time in New England.[5] As one would expect under such circumstances, railroad building was concentrated outside the slave area, but there was some in the South. In 1860 national railroad mileage totaled 30,636, of which almost 11,000 was in the South.[6]

The population density of the South was very much lower than that of the North—in the pre-Civil War decade Virginia had a population density of 14 per square mile as compared with 127 per square mile in Massachusettes—but still there were cities in the South and some of them were quite large. Indeed, of the dozen most populous American cities in 1860, four were in the slave area—Baltimore, New Orleans, St. Louis, and Louisville—and these ranked third, fifth, seventh and eleventh, respectively, Louisville having 68,000 inhabitants and Baltimore 212,000. Other Southern cities, like Charleston, Richmond, Mobile and Norfolk, had considerable populations for their day with a high concentration of working people.[7]

The leading industries in the slave South were flour, lumber, and tobacco. Of consequence, too, were the textile, iron, leather, and turpentine industries. Mining of gold and coal, the manufacturing of hemp and the production of cotton gins likewise were of some importance in the South. The skills and tasks connected with the shipping of goods in such ocean and river ports as New Orleans, Mobile, Wilmington, and Memphis also required thousands of working people.

The data show the industrial development of the slave South, then, to have been on a quite rudimentary level, with processing plants and transportation the major areas of employment of the nascent working class. This backwardness was due, of course, to the overwhelmingly slave-plantation economy of the South.

Nevertheless, we do find in this predominantly agrarian slave South, quite a few cities, some industry, a fairly well-developed transportation system, and the existence of a significant class of workers in factories, aboard ships, at ports, on railroads and canals, and as mechanics, artisans, and unskilled laborers. Many of these workers and artisans were slaves—owned or hired by their employers—and many were free workers (including free Negroes). In addition, during the seventeenth and eighteenth centuries, many workers were in a stage between chattel enslavement and wage employment, i.e., they were indentured servants, laboring, without pay, for a limited number of years.

The slaves, both the minority in the cities and the majority on the plantations, struggled fiercely for freedom, in ways ranging from individual flight to collective uprising.[8] Great militancy also characterized the behavior of the indentured servants, Negro and white, of the South.[9]

And the free Southern urban worker organized and struggled, economically and politically, to improve his conditions. He did this gropingly, on the whole, and he was beset by serious confusions and limitations, but that he did it at all, in the face of the existence of slavery, attests to his courage, to the inexorable quality of working-class organization and to the irreconcilable nature of class conflict between worker and capitalist.

Collective activity and struggle on the part of the working people in the United States dates back to the eighteenth century, and some of these pioneer strivings occurred in the South.

A generation prior to the Revolution, skilled Southern workers in several cities protested the competitive use of slaves and demanded that this cease, a recurrent theme in Southern labor history.[10] During this period there is record of at least one case of collective effort on the part of workers to raise their pay. This involved free Negro chimney sweepers of Charleston who, in 1763, "had the insolence" as the city's *Gazette* put it, "by a combination amongst themselves, to raise the usual prices, and to refuse doing their work, unless their exorbitant demands are complied with." Such activities, continued the paper, "are evils that require some attention to suppress," but just what was the outcome of this particular effort is not known.[11]

Societies of mechanics, artisans and other workers, that played so important a part in the origins and organizational features of the Revolution itself, existed in the South as well as elsewhere. One such society, the Charles Town Mechanics Society, for example, formed the backbone of the South Carolina "Liberty Party" which, as early as 1766, urged American independence.[12]

The immediate post-revolutionary period was marked by the formation of numerous workingmen's benevolent societies and the beginning of their transformation into weapons for increasing wages and otherwise improving working conditions, that is, into trade unions. Once again, this movement was by no means confined to the North. On the contrary, the 1780s and 1790s saw bakers, bricklayers, carpenters, and other skilled workers actively campaigning, in collective fashion, for increased pay in Virginia and the Carolinas. Such groups and such efforts faced, in addition to employer resistance, legal prosecution, as when, in 1783, the carpenters and bricklayers of Charleston were charged with conspiracy because they had combined for the purpose of raising their wages. Bakers of Charleston struck in 1786, while that city's famous Mechanics' Society demanded higher pay in 1794.[13]

At about the same time a Society of Journeymen Tailors was formed in Baltimore, and there is record of a strike conducted by it at least as early as 1795. The central issue was the rate of wages, and in this case an increase was won. Seamen in Baltimore also succeeded in winning a pay raise, by a strike, in 1795.[14]

Nationally, the firm beginnings of an organized labor movement date from the nineteenth century, and this is as true of the South as of the rest of the nation. Leading in this development were the workers of Baltimore—third most populous city in the country prior to the Civil War and while a border city rather than characteristically Southern, still one in which slavery was significant. The printers of Baltimore were organized by 1803, while its tailors conducted successful strikes for higher wages in 1805, 1807, and 1808. The cordwainers (shoemakers) were also quite active during these years and attempted by a strike, in 1809, to obtain a closed shop. The effort failed, and thirty-nine of their leaders were arrested and tried for conspiracy. The records in these cases are poorly preserved, but it appears that one of the workers was found guilty, while the others were acquitted. Seamen successfully struck for higher pay in Baltimore in 1805 and 1807.[15]

Other bits of evidence demonstrate the existence of similar trends at this time elsewhere in the South. Thus, it is clear that a Mechanics' Society was formed in 1806 in New Orleans and the same city witnessed, four years later, the establishment of a typographical workers' union. Again, Charleston carpenters were organized by 1809, and in 1811 there existed a journeymen cordwainers' union in Lexington, Kentucky.[16]

The Second War for Independence waged against England, 1812–15, and the policies and legislation associated with that war, produced a considerable spurt in industrialization. This process continued in the postwar years and helped stimulate mass political activity. It helped lay the groundwork, too, for an aroused labor consciousness in the twenties and thirties. This development did not skip the South.

Indicative is the fact that labor newspapers, which now made their initial appearance, were published in the South as well as elsewhere. First among them was the *Southern Free Press* issued in Charleston in 1825. Within the next decade labor papers appeared in Delaware, Maryland, Missouri, Virginia, Alabama, and Louisiana.[17]

Labor organization went ahead. Charleston clerical workers had formed their own society by 1825. Four years later some 250 Baltimore weavers struck against wage reductions. Their leaders were arrested and tried for conspiracy, but they won an acquittal.[18] Trade unions were, in fact, common in the South by the 1830s. Before the end of the decade, the printers of Columbia, Charleston, Augusta, Louisville, St. Louis, Richmond, Nashville, Natchez, Jacksonville, and Tallahassee were organized. Strikes for higher wages were conducted at this time by these workers in Richmond, Louisville, and New Orleans.[19]

In the early thirties there were at least seven trade unions in Louisville and an even greater number in Baltimore. In the latter city a strike of journeymen hatters against a wage reduction led, in 1833, to a widespread sympathy strike. This, in turn, precipitated the formation of a Union Trade Society having seventeen associated unions—one of the first central trades unions in the United States. This organization was among the pioneers in the demand for the ten-hour day, central to the entire labor movement at the time, and also in making common cause with women workers, for a union of women needleworkers joined the Union Trade Society in 1834. Earlier, in October 1833, these women, organized in the Female Union Society of Tailoresses and Seamstresses, had struck for higher wages, supported by the Journeymen Tailors.[20]

By this time strong organizations of workers existed in St. Louis. Among those having trade unions were the printers, carpenters, plasterers, joiners, cabinet makers. tinners, and barbers. St. Louis cabinet makers struck in 1837, without success, for a raise, but the same year the plasterers, led by Henry B. Miller, won their demand for $2.50 per day.

The workers of St. Louis annually took to the streets in massive parades, on July 4th, in which were raised demands for higher wages and, particularly, the ten-hour day. Other major workers' demonstrations occurred in this decade in Southern cities, notably the mass meeting held in the New Orleans public square in 1835 protesting against the use of slave labor. This significant demonstration was dispersed by the state militia at the governor's order.[21]

It is the thirties, too, which witness the real beginnings of the railroad and canal network binding together the United States. The workers who built these means of transportation under brutal conditions of exploitation (some were slaves), were far from docile, and their militancy was demonstrated in the South, as elsewhere.

One of the first Southern railroads was the Charleston and Hamburg, and its construction workers struck in 1832, only to be crushed by the militia. Again, in 1836, the workers laying the trackage of the Wilmington and Susquehanna struck in Chestertown, Maryland. Before this bid for better working conditions was broken by railroad-hired thugs and militia, five workers were killed and ten wounded.[22]

Strikes and outbreaks, reaching near insurrectionary proportions, marked the building in Maryland of the Chesapeake and Ohio Canal. From 1834 through 1839, the workers struck repeatedly, despite company spies and armed terror. (This included, in 1834, the use of Federal troops—the first time such troops were used as strikebreakers. See: R. B. Morris, in *The American Historical Review,* October 1949.) Typical was this report in a Baltimore publication of the time (*Niles' Weekly Register,* Feb. 21, 1835):

> There has been another riot on the Chesapeake and Ohio canal.... Many laborers, on a certain section, turned-out for higher wages, and would neither work themselves, nor let others work. A troop of horse, and a company of riflemen, with directions to use force to preserve public peace, happily reduced the rioters to order, and drove them away. To refuse such persons employment is the surest way to check a riotous spirit.

This by no means, however, cowed the workers. Sporadic strikes occurred in the following months, to be capped by a great stoppage of work in the summer of 1838. The state militia was ordered out again, but some refused to serve as strikebreakers and a few actually threatened to fight on the side of the workers. In August 1838 an increase in pay was granted, but 130 especially militant workers were fired. A year later another mass strike occurred near Cumberland, Maryland, which was broken by the arrest of 30 leaders and their being sentenced to prison terms ranging from one to eighteen years.[23]

Similarly, hard struggles marked the James River and Kanawha Company's canal-building near Richmond in 1838. Here were employed 500 workers, of whom about 150 were slaves, the rest white wage workers. In May and June the hired workers struck, demanding higher wages, but the strike was broken when most of those out were fired and replaced by 300 slaves. There are also somewhat vague evidences of strikes among the workers of the Central Railroad of Georgia in 1841 and the South Carolina Canal and Railroad in 1845.[24]

Further examples of Southern working-class activity in the forties come from Missouri, Louisiana, and Virginia. Workers in Missouri centered their efforts at this time around the demand for the ten-hour day. More or less sporadic meetings around this theme developed into great labor conventions which, in turn, gave birth to working-class political parties of considerable influence in Missouri during the decade.

Thus, in March 1840, journeymen brickmakers met in St. Louis, pledged to combat vigorously capital's encroachments, "as a duty to ourselves, our families, and our posterity," and announced their adherence to the Ten-Hour System. A labor convention with delegates from twenty-three crafts and occupations assembled in the same city on July 2, 1840, and resolved to fight for the ten-hour day. (These included boatmen, bookbinders, blacksmiths, bricklayers, cabinet-makers, carpenters, carters, coachmen, drayers, hatters, laborers, lime-burners, machinists, painters, plasterers, saddlers, sheet-metal workers, ship carpenters, shoemakers, silversmiths, stonemasons, tailors, and tobacco workers.) From this developed the short-lived, but powerful, Mechanics' and Workingmen's Party of Missouri. Strikes were also resorted to by these workers during this period, the most notable occurring in 1845 when the shipworkers of St. Louis struck for higher wages and won.[25]

In the same decade, in Louisville, Kentucky, the bricklayers organized with the objective of achieving the ten-hour day but, facing the competition of slaves, they failed. So, also—and for the same reason—did the carpenters and painters of that city fail in a strike for a shorter work day, but the stonecutters, without slave competition, succeeded in gaining the ten-hour day.[26]

Mechanics and printers in New Orleans and Baton Rouge participated in active struggles during the forties. Outstanding was the action of Baton Rouge mechanics in leaving their city in protest against the competitive use of convict labor, an action which resulted in the elimination of the grievance in 1845.[27]

One of the most important of pre-Civil War strikes occurred in Richmond in 1847. This took place in the South's leading iron mill, the Tredegar Iron Works. The white workers, led by one named Gatewood Talley, demanded a raise in wages and the abandonment of the use of slaves in the plant. The press of the city and the region was particularly vicious in combatting this strike, denouncing it as akin to abolitionism (i.e., in their eyes, treason) and as threatening to "wholly destroy the value of slave property."

The strikers, occupying company-owned houses, were evicted, the leaders arrested, at the mayor's order, on the charge of conspiracy, and additional slave workers were purchased and hired (that is, rented from their masters). After weeks of resistance, these strike-breaking measures succeeded, and thereafter this iron mill operated, until and through the Civil War, very largely with slave labor. The slaves, themselves, caused keen concern for the boss, especially because of frequent flight.[28]

A somewhat similar event occurred the same year on a Louisiana sugar plantation. A slaveowner replaced his unfree labor force with about one hundred Irish and German immigrants. An English visitor reported the result:

> In the middle of the harvest they all struck for double pay. No others were to be had, and it was impossible to purchase slaves in a few days. In that short time he lost produce to the value of ten thousand dollars.

The planter returned to slave labor.[29]

Workers were markedly militant during the 1850s in several Southern states. Thus, about 1850, the cotton screwmen of New Orleans, (workers who, using large jackscrews, packed cotton bales into the holds of ships), organized the Screwmen's Beneficial Association, and conducted successful strikes for higher wages in 1854 and 1858. By 1860 practically all the workers of that craft in New Orleans were unionized. Seamen and longshoremen in the same city struck repeatedly for better pay in 1851 and 1852. There is evidence also of the existence of Agricultural and Mechanical Societies, as well as Mechanics' Societies in Baton Rouge and New Orleans during the same period, and these represented additional forms of worker organization.[30]

In 1852 the New Orleans Typographical Union was reorganized (under the leadership of Gerard Stith, later mayor of the city) and greatly strengthened. The next year the members struck against the city's newspapers, and although strikebreakers were imported from

New York City, the determination of the local workers remained firm. Their efforts were successful and a raise of 25 percent was won.[31]

In 1857 under the leadership of Richard Trevellick, who had been active in the struggle for an eight-hour day in his native Australia (and was to be a very important post-Civil War labor leader), the ship carpenters and caulkers of New Orleans formed a union. This succeeded in obtaining a nine-hour day for its members. Longshoremen and deckhands, undoubtedly stimulated by all this activity, themselves took the road of organization, also in the fifties. Strikes by these workers occurred frequently and, in 1858 the slave state of Louisiana passed a law prohibiting strikes or work stoppages on ships or at freight wharves.[32] Arrests as a result of this law were common in Louisiana for several years thereafter. Roger Shugg, in his pioneering work, *Origins of Class Struggle in Louisiana* (Baton Rouge, 1939), wrote: "The free worker in New Orleans was in danger of losing his freedom and being pulled into the orbit of slavery."[33]

There is a record of the unionization of carpenters in Hopkinsville, Ashland, and Paducah, Kentucky; and of typographical workers in Memphis and Nashville, Tennessee, Raleigh, North Carolina, and Petersburg, Virginia, in the 1850s.[34] Petersburg was the scene of another example of labor activity in 1854. The owner of a sawmill near that city called for a longer work day. The workers struck, threatened to ride the boss on a rail, and marched in a protest demonstration to the city. There was no increase in hours.[35]

An inconclusive strike of typographical workers occurred in Charleston, South Carolina in 1853, and in 1857 the workers in William Gregg's loudly ballyhooed "model" textile mill in Graniteville, of the same state, struck for higher wages. Here, too, the result is not on record.[36]

At the same time iron molders in the South were organizing. Southern locals of the National Molders Union, led by William H. Sylvis— later, founder of the National Labor Union—were formed in the fifties in Richmond, Memphis, St. Louis, Baltimore and Louisville. In several instances, as in St. Louis in 1858 and in Baltimore in 1860, hard-fought strikes were conducted.[37]

Another pioneer national trade union, the American Miners' Association, parent of the U.M.W.A., had some of its roots in a slave state. Two strikes of miners occurred in the 1850s in the Cumberland coalfield in Maryland, where about 350 men worked. In 1850–51, these men struck for six weeks against the bosses' demand for a wage cut and an agreement barring work stoppages. The workers won. In 1854, however, the workers lost in their demand for 40 cents a ton of coal (they accepted 30 cents) after being out fourteen weeks and facing the armed might of the state militia. There is a direct line connecting these militant actions and the formation in 1861 of the American Miners' Association.[38]

The decade of the fifties was marked, too, by several strikes among Southern railroad workers. Notable was the strike in South Carolina, early in 1855, of workers employed by the North Eastern Railroad. The men sought to increase their pay from $1 per day to $1.25, but the state crushed it by arresting twenty-three of the leaders, charging them with "inspiring terror" and seeking "an unlawful end." All were fined and jailed.[39] More successful was the effort of the workers in Memphis employed by the Memphis & Charleston Railroad. In 1860 these workers felt sufficiently well organized to demand a one-hour reduction in their eleven-hour day. After prolonged struggles, marked by large-scale demonstrations and public meetings, the workers won their demands.[40]

Marxism appeared in the United States during the decade prior to the Civil War, and its influence was felt in that period in the South as well as the North.[41] William Z. Foster, in his *History of the Communist Party of the United States* (p. 39) points to the heroic anti-slavery activity of Marxists in the South, such as Adolph Douai in Texas and Hermann Meyer in Alabama. Their activity, however, was not confined to opposition to slavery. They were Marxists and so, while of course fighting against slavery, the central task of the time, they also projected programs and participated in efforts of the working class as such.

There were Marxist groups, overwhelmingly German in composition, in Maryland, Virginia, Kentucky, Missouri, Louisiana, and Texas. Out of a total of 600,000 people in Texas in 1860, over 20,000 were Germans, living in the western part of the state and shunning the employment of slave labor. To many of these settlers, and especially to the large segment among them who were political refugees from the 1848 revolution, Marxism was more or less familiar.

In the early fifties Marxist clubs and organizations had appeared amongst these German settlers in Texas, and in 1853 Adolph Douai began publishing the *San Antonio Zeitung, ein Sozial-Demokratisches Blatt fur die Deutschen in West Texas. (San Antonio Times,* a Social-

Democratic newspaper for the Germans in West Texas.) By 1854, the *Austin State Times* (May 19) was delicately hinting: "The contiguity of the San Antonio River to the *Zeitung* office, we think suggests the suppression of that paper. Pitch in."[42]

Two years later—a time of tremendous slave unrest throughout the South—though the press itself was not destroyed, Douai was forced, in peril of his life, to flee the South. It was the whole democratic orientation of his paper, its firm espousal of the abolition of slavery, and its Marxist approach, which produced its forcible suppression by the Texas slaveowners.[43]

In 1850 a German Workmen's Convention met in Philadelphia. The Marxist influence at this gathering was potent. Its forty-four delegates, each representing 100 workers, discussed trade union and political perspectives. Of the six cities sending delegates, three—St. Louis, Baltimore and Louisville—were in the slave area.[44] The next year a German Social-Democratic Association was founded in Richmond which remained of sufficient consequence, during the fifties, to be denounced intermittently by the local press.[45] Similarly, it is of some interest to note that Senator Robert Toombs of Georgia turned to red-baiting and anti-Semitism in his 1853 campaign, announcing that his opponents were not merely tools of the Abolitionists, but were also "German Jews [and] Red Republicans."[46]

A radical German-language newspaper, showing distinct Marxist influence, *Der Wecker* (The Awakener) was established in Baltimore by Carl Heinrich Schnauffer, poet, 1848 revolutionist, and political refugee. This paper called for the organization of trade unions, an eight-hour day, universal suffrage, and the abolition of slavery. After Schnauffer's death in 1854 his wife edited the paper for three years, when Wilhelm Rapp, another '48er, and president of Baltimore's *Turnerbund*, became editor. He continued its politically advanced policies, and supported Lincoln in the election of 1860. In April 1861 a mob drove Rapp out of Baltimore, but Mrs. Schnauffer heroically and successfully defended the press, and continued the paper's publication.[47]

A newspaper of similar character was founded by another '48er in Louisville in 1854. The *Herold des Westens*, edited by Karl Heinzen (an early associate of Marx who later turned against Marxism), denounced slavery, called for "the protection of the laboring classes from the capitalists" and advocated universal suffrage, including the enfranchisement of women. It demanded the enactment of minimum wage and maximum hour laws, and the granting, without charge, of public lands to bonafide settlers. A like-inclined newspaper, the *Deutsche Zeitung,* appeared about this time in New Orleans[48] and boldly supported "Free Soil, Free Speech, Free Men, and Fremont" [the Republican presidential candidate] in the election of 1856.

The program of the Richmond Social-Democratic Association, as put forth in 1854, survives and no doubt epitomizes the program of Marxist, and near-Marxist, Southern groups prior to the Civil War. This association demanded the emancipation of the slaves, the wide dispersal of land ownership, the nationalization of the railroads, "the amelioration of the condition of the working class," by providing an eight-hour day for adults and a five-hour day for children, by the development of trade unions and workingmen's societies, by a mechanics' lien law, free public education, abolition of imprisonment for debt, and a revision of the system of taxation so that it would be based on the capacity to pay. It advocated the popular election of all officeholders by universal suffrage, with the power of recall vested in the electorate.[49]

Of course, the labor movement in the South was still in its elementary stages and is not to be thought of as offering anything like decisive weight in the whole Southern struggle against the Bourbon oligarchy. This struggle was waged in the main by the Negro masses and by the non-slaveholding whites who made their bare and precarious living by tilling the soil.

However, among these non-slaveholding whites of country and city, racism was rampant. It was the single most important ideological instrument the Bourbons had for the maintenance of their system. This helped make impossible any fully effective struggle against the ruling class on the part of its victims. It prevented the non-slaveholding whites, in factory or farm, from developing a policy and a program in cooperation with the Negro people that might have resulted in actually defeating the slaveowners.

Yet, the marked militancy of Southern wage workers in the 1850s is part of the whole pattern of increased opposition to slavocratic domination which is so significant a component of Southern history in the pre-Civil War decade. Other aspects of this developing threat to Bourbon power in terms of rising slave disaffection, numerous instances of Negro-white unity in slave plots and uprisings, and the economic and political opposition of non-slaveholding whites (urban and rural) to the planters' dictatorship, together with the reasons therefore, have been examined elsewhere.[50]

The Bourbons met these threats with increasingly harsh repression, and they followed the same course in meeting the appearance and development of working-class organization and activity. In a slave society, labor was considered loathsome, and the ruling class of the American slave society detested and feared working people. "Free society!" exclaimed a Georgia newspaper in 1856, "we sicken at the name. What is it but a conglomeration of greasy mechanics, filthy operatives, smallfisted farmers, and moon-struck theorists?" Merchants and capitalists, said a South Carolina newspaper during the same period, were not unduly hostile to a slaveholding society, "but the mechanics, most of them, are pests to society, dangerous among the slave populations and ever ready to form combinations against the interest of the slaveholder, against the laws of the country, and against the peace of Commonwealth."[51]

More and more, in law and in theory and in fact, the rulers of the slave South tried to eliminate the distinction between chattel slavery and wage labor. As we have seen, this led a careful historian of the question in one state (Roger Shugg's study of Louisiana) to write that, in the fifties, the free worker was being pulled more and more "into the orbit of slavery." Long before, contemporaneously, indeed, Karl Marx had stated:

> Between 1856 and 1860 the political spokesmen, jurists, moralists and theologians of the slaveholders' party had already sought to prove not so much that Negro slavery is justified, but rather that color is a matter of indifference, and the working class is everywhere born to slavery.[52]

The facts concerning the organizational efforts of Southern free workers, and the bitter resistance to these efforts by the Southern rulers, give added substance to Marx's fundamental evaluation of the Civil War:

> The present struggle between the South and the North is, therefore, nothing but a struggle between two social systems, between the system of slavery and the system of free labor.[53]

The Southern masses, Negro and white, hated the Bourbons. This hatred intensified as the slave system aged and became increasingly oligarchic and tyrannical. It is, in part, this increasing disaffection of the home population which drove the slaveowning class to the desperate expedient of seeking, forcibly, to overthrow the government of the

United States—to defy the election results of 1860 and to retain their paramount power, in the South at least, by armed secession.

Just as fear and hatred of the masses in the South was consequential in moving the slaveholders to undertake their armed counter-revolutionary attempt, so the masses' hatred for those slaveholders was of great consequence in helping to defeat that attempt. Secession was accomplished against the will of the vast majority of Southern people, and the collapse of the Confederacy was due not only to the pounding of the Union forces (in which, by the way, served scores of thousands of Southerners, Negro and white), and to the superiority of the Union's industrial might and population potential. That collapse, complete as it was, cannot be understood if one does not understand that the Confederacy never had the devotion of the majority of Southerners. The Negro masses, 35 percent of the South's total population, detested the Confederacy as the instrument of their enslavers, and their activity in opposition to that government and in support of Lincoln's was of fundamental importance in the Confederacy's defeat.

Moreover, most of the Southern white masses opposed the Confederacy and this, too, was fundamental in explaining its collapse. Over 110,000 soldiers deserted the Confederate army, many taking their guns with them. Most of these men successfully resisted recapture because of the people's sympathy and assistance, and many in organized detachments offered battle to regular units of the Confederate army. Major cities were besieged by these Southern opponents of Jefferson Davis' government, and other areas of the South, particularly in the mountain districts, never were won over to secession. Other forms of disaffection among the white masses had devastating effects upon the strength and stability of the Davis regime. These included, most notably, the so-called Bread Riots, led by impoverished working women, in Virginia, North Carolina and Alabama. Here hundreds, and, at time, thousands of women (and, seeing their example, some men) gathered together and marched, armed with clubs, etc., upon stores and helped themselves to food for their starving families. In other cases army commissary supplies, and even army supplies in transit, were forcibly taken by Southern women facing destitution in the "rich man's war and the poor man's fight" that the slaveowners had launched.

Of great consequence, too, were the numerous Peace, and Union Societies which sprang up by the hundreds throughout the South. These became more and more numerous as the slaughter continued.

Their political influence in large areas of the Confederacy was potent and continued to mount throughout the war.[54] It was the poor, in countryside and city, who formed the mass base of these groups.

Part of this larger story is the fact that the trade-union and organizational stirrings of Southern workers, which, as we have seen, were present in the pre-Civil War generation and reached a high point in the fifties, continued during the Civil War itself. We turn, then, to a consideration of Southern labor activity during the war years.

The necessities of fighting led to the development of industrialization in the South during the war. As a result, additional thousands of workers, including many women, appeared. These workers, plagued by an inflation which far outstripped occasional and tiny wage increases, often turned to organization and sometimes to strikes in order to force some improvements in starvation conditions. While this militancy appears, the presence of slavery—during the war years, as before—prevented the workers from really breaking through and achieving thorough organization or substantial gains.

The workers could and did withstand court processes, frame-ups, violence and even impressment into the army—all these methods were used by the bosses to break up the workers' organizational efforts. But the workers could not overcome the bosses' prime weapon, slavery. The impressment of slaves into ordnance works, railroads (slaves were used in all positions, including those of brakemen and firemen), maritime, and some factory work could, and did, vanquish war-time struggles of the free workers. Never more vividly than during the Civil War, in the South, was confirmed the truth of Marx's statement: "Labor cannot emancipate itself in the white skin where in the black skin it is branded."

The reports of Southern strikes during the Civil War are exceedingly fragmentary, and undoubtedly many went completely unrecorded. Still enough is at hand to show that wage workers of the South struggled militantly during the war to better their conditions.

During the first year of the fighting, workers in the Confederacy's largest ironworks—the Tredegar plant in Richmond—struck for higher wages, but the outcome of this struggle is not known. In 1862 several strikes were reported in Secessia's capital city, including among harness workers, lithographers, typographers and cemetery workers. The cemetery workers were fired and replaced by slaves; the lithographers and typographers saw their leaders arrested and jailed for "conspiracy" and this broke their effort; the outcome in the case of the harness workers is not known. Machinists in the shops of the Virginia & Tennessee Railroad in Lynchburg also went on strike in 1862. Their strike was broken when the Confederacy conscripted the strikers into the army.

Conscription also broke a strike of the workers in the Richmond armory in 1863, while the outcome of the strike of shoemakers in that city the same year is unknown. One of the few successful strikes during the war was carried out in 1863 in Richmond, by women workers employed in the Confederate States Laboratory. These workers won a wage increase, but when they struck again in 1864, all were fired. A strike for higher pay by the Confederate postal clerks was partially successful, some increase being obtained.[55]

Machinists, smiths, and other workers at the armory in Macon, Georgia, and at the Shelby Iron Company in Columbiana, Georgia, went on strike in 1863 for a wage increase. In both cases the outcome is uncertain. In March 1864 the chief of the Macon armory informed General Josiah Gorgas, over-all commander of Confederate ordnance, that the workers "generally were so much dissatisfied with the wages allowed them that it is impossible to get them to apply themselves to their work in anything like a satisfactory manner." By May 1864 the wage workers in this Macon armory were again ready to strike and now the situation was met by replacing all of them with requisitioned slave laborers.[56] During the same period workers struck at the Naval Ordnance Works in Atlanta. They demanded higher pay, but once again, the outcome is not clear from available records.[57]

One of the most extensive and best organized strikes among Southern workers in the Confederacy involved telegraph operators, civil and military. These workers announced in October 1863 the formation of a Confederate-wide Southern Telegraphic Association, the leading officers of which were Charles A. Gaston of Mobile, J. S. Clarke of Charleston, C. F. Barnes of Augusta, and W. H. Clarke of Savannah.

The telegraph operators worked six days a week from 7 in the morning to 10 in the evening, and put in 4 hours on Sunday—*i.e.,* a 94-hour week! They declared, when announcing the existence of their Association, that, "Our rights have not been respected by the various telegraph companies, and they have recently used the conscript law of the Confederate States as a means to intimidate us to succumb to demands we consider unfair and tyrannical." The bosses remained adamant and telegraph operators throughout the Confederacy struck in January 1864 for a closed shop, higher pay, and a shorter work day.

The slavocrat press denounced the workers as conspirators and traitors and urged that all of them be drafted and then, in uniform, returned to their jobs.[58] Exactly this was done, after the men had held firm for a month. They were conscripted and forced to work at pay that equalled seventeen (Confederate) dollars a month![59]

The last session of the Confederate Congress had under consideration several bills which outlawed strikes and trade unions entirely, or any kind of collective activity on the part of wage workers. There is no doubt that had the war continued another year such legislation would have been passed by the Davis regime, enemy that the regime was to human freedom in general.

Hitherto it has been generally held that the labor movement by-passed the slave South. It is certainly true that the slave South was overwhelmingly agrarian and this itself limited the possibility of a major labor movement. It is also true that the existence of slavery militated against the development of a numerous working class in the cities, and in any case against the development of a large-scale, effective labor organization. In this sense, a basic lesson of the history of the labor movement in the slave South is the catastrophic cost to the white working population in particular, as well as to the South as a whole, of the enslavement of the Negro people.

Nevertheless, to see the picture in its entirety, it is important to understand that cities and ports, railroads and canals, factories and mines did exist in the slave South, and that these were made useful and productive, there as everywhere, by working men and women, among whom were wage workers as well as slaves. These free workers, facing the exploitation of their bosses, did organize to oppose or to limit their exploitation.

In the slave South trade unions were formed, strikes were conducted, and a labor press and labor parties were brought into being. In the slave South, Marxists and bourgeois-democratic revolutionaries (many of them very much influenced by Marxism) lived and worked. Marxism helped plant the seed of class consciousness, independent political action and Negro-white unity in the pre-Civil War South.

This working-class movement is part of the opposition to slavocrat domination which is so decisive a part of Southern history. Its upsurge in the 1850s is part, too, of the rising threat to Bourbon power which characterizes the pre-Civil War decade and strongly affected ruling-class policy. And labor unrest and militancy are facets of the mass opposition within the South, to the slaveholders' Confederate government, an opposition of fundamental consequence in causing that government's collapse.

Finally, the history of labor struggles in the slave South is a precious part of the entire and continuing effort of the American working class to fully and effectively organize itself. It is part of the not-to-be-denied struggle of the American working class, the Negro people, the farming, and toiling masses generally, to produce a United States of equality, security, democracy, and peace for all.

Published as a pamphlet, *The Labor Movement in the South During Slavery* (New York: International Publishers, 1954).

Class Conflicts in the South: 1850-1860

The great attention given to the spectacular political struggles between the North and the South in the decade before the Civil War has tended to befog the equally important contests which went on during the same period within the South itself.

Writers have dealt at considerable length with the national scene, have demonstrated a growing conflict between an agrarian, slave-labor society and an increasingly industrial, free-labor society as to which should direct public opinion, enact and administer the laws, appropriate the West—in short, which should control the state. In 1860 the grip of the slave civilization upon the national government was very considerably loosened and clearly seemed destined to complete annihilation. The slavocracy therefore turned to bullets.

But there was more to it than that. The facts are that not only did the slavocrats see their external, or national, power seriously menaced by the Republican triumph of 1860, but they also observed their internal, local power greatly threatened by increasing restlessness among the exploited classes—the non-slaveholding whites and the slaves.

There were three general manifestations of this unrest: (1) slave disaffection, shown in individual acts of "insolence" or terrorism, and in concerted, planned efforts for liberation; (2) numerous instances of poor-white implication in the slave conspiracies and revolts, showing a declining efficiency in the divide-and-rule policy of the Bourbons; (3) independent political action of the non-slaveholding whites aimed at the destruction of the slavocracy's control of the state governments. This growing internal disaffection is a prime explanation for the desperation of the slaveholding class which drove it to the expedient of civil war.

Factors tending to explain the slave unrest of the decade are soil exhaustion, leading to greater work demands, improved marketing facilities, having the same result, and economic depression, 1854-56, throughout the South, approaching, especially in 1855, the famine stage. These years witnessed, too, a considerable increase in industrialization and urbanization within the South. These phenomena[1] were distinctly not conducive to the creation of happy slaves. As a slaveholder remarked,[2] "The cities is no place for niggers. They get strange notions into their heads, and grow discontented. They ought, every one of them, to be sent back to the plantations." As a matter of fact there was for this reason, during this decade, an attempt to foster a "back-to-the-plantation" movement.

It is also true, as Frederick L. Olmsted observed,[3] that: "Any great event having the slightest bearing upon the question of emancipation is known to produce an unwholesome excitement" among the slaves. The decade is characterized by such events as the 1850 Compromise, the sensation caused by *Uncle Tom's Cabin,* the Kansas War, the 1856 election, the Dred Scott decision, Helper's *Impending Crisis,* John Brown's raid, and the election of 1860. If to this is added the political and social struggles within the South itself (to be described later), it becomes apparent that there were many occasions for "unwholesome excitement."

Combined with all this is a significant change in the Abolitionist movement. Originally this aimed at gradual emancipation induced by moral suasion. Then came the demand for immediate liberation, but still only via moral suasion. Then followed a split into those favoring political action and those opposed. Finally, and most noticeably in this decade, there arose a body of direct actionists whose idea was to "carry the war into Africa."

The shift is exemplified in the person of Henry C. Wright. In the forties he wrote the "Non-Resistant" column for Garrison's *Liberator*. By 1851 he felt it was the duty of Abolitionists to go South and aid the slaves to flee, and by 1859 he was convinced[4] that it was "the right and duty of the slaves to resist their masters, and the right and duty of the North to incite them to resistance, and to aid them." By November 1856, Frederick Douglass was certain that the "peaceful annihilation" of slavery was "almost hopeless" and therefore contended[5] "that the slave's right to revolt is perfect, and only wants the occurrence of favorable circumstances to become a duty. . . . We cannot but shudder as we call to mind the horrors that have marked servile insurrections— we would avert them if we could; but shall the millions for ever submit to robbery, to murder, to ignorance, and every unnamed evil which an irresponsible tyranny can devise, because the overthrow of that tyranny would be productive of horrors? We say not . . . terrible as it will be, we accept and hope for it."

And while John Brown's work was the most spectacular, he was by no means the only Northern man to agitate among the slaves themselves; there were others, the vast majority unnamed, but some are known, like Alexander Ross, James Redpath, and W. L. Chaplin.[6] But this exceedingly dangerous work was mainly done by Northern or Canadian Negroes who had themselves escaped from slavery. A few of these courageous people are known—Harriet Tubman, Josiah Henson, William Still, Elijah Anderson, John Mason. It has been estimated[7] that, from Canada alone, in 1860, 500 Negroes went into the South to rescue their brothers. What people can offer a more splendid chapter to the record of human fortitude?

The obvious is at times elusive and it is therefore necessary to bear in mind when trying to discover the causes of slave disaffection that one is indeed dealing with *slaves*. We will give but one piece of evidence to indicate something of what is meant. In January 1854 the British consul at Charleston, in a private letter, wrote, "The frightful atrocities of slave holding must be seen to be described . . . . My next-door neighbor, a lawyer of the first distinction, and a member of the *Southern Aristocracy*, told me himself that he flogged all his own negroes, men and women, when they misbehaved. . . . It is literally no more to kill a slave than to shoot a dog."[8]

There is considerable evidence pointing to a quite general state of insubordination and disaffection, apart from conspiracies and revolts, among the slave population.

A lady of Burke County, North Carolina, complained in April 1850 of such a condition among her slaves and declared, "I have not a single servant (slave) at my command." Three years later a traveler in the South observed "in the newspapers, complaints of growing insolence and insubordination among the negroes."[9] References to the "common practice with slaves" of harboring runaways recur, as do items of the arrest of slaves caught in the act of learning to read. A paper of 1858 reported the arrest of ninety Negroes for that "crime." It urged severe punishment and remarked, "Scarcely a week passes, that instruments of writing, prepared by negroes, are not taken from servants (slaves) in the streets, by the police."[10]

A Louisiana paper of 1858 reported "more cases of insubordination among the negro population . . . than ever known before," and a Missouri paper of 1859 commented upon the "alarmingly frequent" cases of slaves killing their owners. It added that "retribution seems to be dealt out to the perpetrators with dispatch and in the form to which only a people wrought up to the highest degree of indignation and excitement would resort."[11]

Examples of such retribution with their justification are enlightening. Olmsted tells of the burning of a slave near Knoxville, Tenn., for the offense of killing his master and quotes the editor of a "liberal" newspaper as justifying the lynching as a "means of absolute, necessary self-defense." The same community shortly found six legal executions needed for the stability of its society.[12] Similarly, a slave in August 1854 killed his master in Mt. Meigs, Alabama, and, according to the Vigilance Committee, boasted of his deed. This slave, too, was burned alive. "The gentlemen constituting the meeting were men of prudence, deliberation and intelligence, and acted from an imperative sense of the necessity of an example to check the growing and dangerous insubordination of the slave population." Precisely the same things happened[13] in the same region in June 1856 and January 1857. Again, in August 1855 a patrolman in Louisiana killed a slave who did not stop when hailed and this was considered[14] proper since "Recent disorders among the slaves in New Iberia had made it a matter of importance that the laws relative to the police of slaves, should be strictly enforced."

A common method by which American slaves showed their "docility" was arson. This occurred with striking frequency during the ten years under scrutiny. For example, from Nov. 26, 1850, to Jan. 15, 1851, one New Orleans paper reported slave burnings of at least seven sugar houses. For a similar period, Jan. 31, 1850, to May 30, 1851, there were seven *convictions* of slaves in Virginia for arson.[15]

Burnings were at times concerted. Thus the Norfolk *Beacon* of Sept. 21, 1852, declared that the slaves of Princess Anne County, Va., had excited alarm and that an extra patrol had been ordered out. And,

> On Sunday night last, this patrol made a descent upon a church where a large number of negroes had congregated for the purpose of holding a meeting, and dispersed them. In a short time, the fodder stacks of one of the party who lived near were discovered on fire. The patrol immediately started for the fire, but before reaching the scene it was discovered that the stacks of other neighbors had shared a like fate, all having no doubt been fired by the negroes for revenge. A strict watch is now kept over them, and most rigid means adopted to make every one know and keep his place.

The *Federal Union* of Milledgeville, Ga., of March 20, 1855, told of incendiary fires set by slaves that month in South Carolina and three counties of Georgia. Property damage was considerable and "many persons were seriously injured."[16]

The fleeing of slaves reached very great proportions from 1850 to 1860 and was a constant and considerable source of annoyance to the slavocracy. According to the census estimates 1,011 slaves *succeeded* in escaping in 1850 and 803 *succeeded* in 1860. At current prices that represented a loss of about $1,000,000 each year. But that is a very small part of the story. First, the census reports were poor. The census takers were paid a certain sum for each entrant and so tended to make only those calls that were least expensive to themselves. City figures were therefore more reliable than those for rural communities. Moreover, Olmsted found census taking in the South "more than ordinarily unreliable" and told of a census taker there who announced that he would be at a certain tavern at a certain day "for the purpose of receiving from the people of the vicinity—who were requested to call upon him—the information it was his duty to obtain!"[17]

According to Professor W. B. Hesseltine, "Between 1830 and 1860 as many as 2,000 slaves a year passed into the land of the free along the routes of the Underground Railroad," and Professor Siebert has declared[18] that this railroad saw its greatest activity from 1850 to 1860. And this is just a fraction of those who fled but did not succeed in reaching a free land, who were captured or forced to turn back. When people pay as high as $300 for one bloodhound[19] the fleeing of slaves is a serious problem indeed.

It is also to be noted that the decade witnessed a qualitative as well as quantitative change in the fugitive slave problem, for now not only did more slaves flee, but more often than before they fled in groups; they, as Southern papers put it, stampeded.[20]

Another piece of evidence of the growing unrest of the slave population is afforded by the figures for money appropriated by the state of Virginia for slaves owned by her citizens who were legally executed or banished from the state.[21] For the fiscal year 1851-52 the sum equalled $12,000; for 1852-53 the sum was $15,000; 1853-54, $19,000 was appropriated and the same for 1854-55. For the year 1855-56 $22,000 was necessary and this was duplicated the next year. For 1857-58 the sum was $35,000 and stayed at the same high level for 1858-59. For each of the next two years prior to the Civil War, 1859-60, and 1860-61, $30,000 was appropriated. Thus "bad" slaves, legally disposed of, cost the one state of Virginia in ten years the sum of $239,000.

There was still another manifestation of slave disaffection: conspiracy or revolt. Some of the episodes already described, as that in Virginia in 1852 or in Georgia in 1855, may perhaps be thought of as conspiracies. The decade witnessed many more, the most important of which follow.

A free Negro, George Wright, of New Orleans, was asked by a slave, Albert, in June 1853 to join in a revolt.[22] He declared his interest and was brought to a white man, a teacher by the name of Dyson, who had come to Louisiana in 1840 from Jamaica. Dyson trusted Wright, declared that one hundred whites had agreed to aid the Negroes in their bid for freedom, and urged Wright to join. Wright did—verbally. He almost immediately betrayed the plot and led the police to the slave Albert. The slave at the time of arrest, June 13, carried a knife, a sword, a revolver, one bag of bullets, one pound of powder, two boxes of percussion caps, and $86. The patrol was ordered out, the city guard strengthened, and twenty slaves and Dyson were instantly arrested.

Albert stated that 2,500 slaves were involved. He named none. In prison he declared that "all his friends had gone down the coast and were fighting like soldiers. If he had shed blood in the cause he would not have minded the arrest." It was indeed reported that "a large number of negroes have fled from their masters and are now missing," but no actual fighting was mentioned. Excitement was great along the coast, however, and the arrest of one white man, a cattle driver, occurred at Bonnet Clare. A fisherman, Michael McGill, testified that he had taken Dyson and two slaves carrying what he thought were arms to a swamp from which several Negroes emerged. The Negroes were given the arms and disappeared.

The New Orleans papers tended to minimize the trouble, but did declare that the city contained "malicious and fanatical" whites, "cut-throats in the name of liberty—murderers in the guise of philanthropy" and commended the swift action of the police, while calling for further precautions and restrictions. The last piece of information concerning this is an item telling of an attack by Albert upon the jailer in which he caused "the blood to flow." The disposition of the rebels is not reported.

The year 1856 was one of extraordinary slave unrest. The first serious difficulty of the year was caused by maroons in North Carolina. A letter[23] of August 25, 1856, to Governor Thomas Bragg signed by Richard A. Lewis and twenty-one others informed him of a "very secure retreat for runaway negroes" in a large swamp between Bladen and Robeson Counties. There "for many years past, and at this time, there are several runaways of bad and daring character—destructive to all kinds of Stock and dangerous to all persons living by or near said swamp." Slaveholders attacked these maroons August 1, but accomplished nothing and saw one of their own number killed. "The negroes ran off cursing and swearing and telling them to come on, they were ready for them again." The Wilmington *Journal* of August 14 mentioned that these Negroes "had cleared a place for a garden, had cows, etc., in the swamp." Mr. Lewis and his friends were "unable to offer sufficient inducement for negro hunters to come with their dogs unless aided from other sources." The governor suggested that magistrates call for the militia, but whether this was done or not is unknown.

A plot involving over 200 slaves and supposed to mature on September 6, 1856, was discovered[24] in Colorado County, Texas, shortly before that date. Many of the Mexican inhabitants of the region were declared to be implicated. And it was felt "that the lower class of the Mexican population are incendiaries in any country where slaves are held." They were arrested and ordered to leave the county within five days and never to return "under the penalty of death." A white person by the name of William Mehrmann was similarly dealt with. Arms were discovered in the possession of a few slaves. Every one of the 200 arrested was severely whipped, two dying under the lash. Three were hanged. One slave leader, Frank, was not captured.

Trouble involving some 300 slaves and a few white men, one of whom was named James Hancock, was reported in October from two counties, Ouchita and Union, in Arkansas, and two parishes, Union and Claiborne, across the border in Louisiana. The outcome here is not known. On November 7 "an extensive scheme of negro insurrection" was discovered in Lavaca, De Witt and Victoria Counties in the Southeastern part of Texas and very near Colorado County, seat of the October conspiracy. A letter from Victoria of November 7 declared that: "The negroes had killed off all the dogs in the neighborhood, and were preparing for a general attack" when betrayal came. Whites were implicated, one being "severely horsewhipped," and the others driven out of the county. What became of the slaves is not stated.[25]

One week later a conspiracy was disclosed in St. Mary parish, Louisiana. It was believed[26] that "favorite family servants" were the leaders. Slaves throughout the parish were arrested. Three white men and one free Negro were also held. The slaves were lashed and returned to their masters, but the four others were imprisoned. The local paper of November 22 declared that the free Negro "and at least one of the white men, will suffer death for the part taken in the matter."

And in the very beginning of November trouble was reported[27] from Tennessee. A letter of November 2 told of the arrest of thirty slaves, and a white man named Williams, in Fayette County, at the Southwestern tip of the state. It was believed that the plot extended to "the surrounding counties and states." Confirmation of this soon came. Within two weeks unrest was reported from Montgomery County in the north central part of the state, and across the border in the iron foundries of Louisa, Kentucky. Again many slaves and one white man were arrested. Shortly thereafter plots were discovered in Obion, at Tennessee's western tip, and in Fulton, Kentucky, as well as in New Madrid and Scott Counties, Missouri.

In December, plots were reported, occasionally outbreaks occurred, and slaves and whites were arrested, tortured, banished and executed in virtually every slave state. The discontent forced its way through, notwithstanding clear evidences of censorship. Thus a Georgia paper confessed that slave disaffection was a "delicate subject to touch" and that it had "refrained from giving our readers any of the accounts of contemplated insurrections."[28]

The Washington correspondent of the New York *Weekly Tribune* declared on December 20 that: "The insurrectionary movement in

Tennessee obtained more headway than is known to the public—important facts being suppressed in order to check the spread of the contagion and prevent the true condition of affairs from being understood elsewhere." Next week the same correspondent stated that he had "reliable information" of serious trouble in New Orleans leading to the hanging of twenty slaves, "but the newspapers carefully refrain from any mention of the facts."

Indeed, the New Orleans *Daily Picayune* of December 9 had itself admitted that it had "refrained from publishing a great deal which we receive by the mails, going to show that there is a spirit of turbulence abroad in various quarters." December 23 it said the same thing about "this very delicate subject" but did state that there were plots for rebellion during the Christmas holidays "in Kentucky, Arkansas and Tennessee, as well as in Mississippi, Louisiana and Texas" and that recent events "along the Cumberland river in Kentucky and Tennessee and the more recent affairs in Mississippi, approach very nearly to positive insurrection."

To this may be added Maryland, Alabama, Virginia, North Carolina, South Carolina, Georgia and Florida.[29] Features of the conspiracies are worth particular notice. Arms were discovered among the slaves in, at least, Tennessee, Kentucky and Texas. Preparations for blowing up bridges were uncovered. Attacks upon iron mills in Kentucky were started but defeated. At least three whites were killed by slaves in that same state. The date for the execution of four slaves in Dover, Tennessee, was pushed ahead for fear of an attempt at rescue, and a body of 150 men was required to break up a group of about the same number of slaves marching to Dover for that very purpose.

Free Negroes were directly implicated as well as slaves in Kentucky, and they were driven out of several cities as Murfreesboro, Tenn., Paducah, Ky., and Montgomery, Ala. Whites, too, were often implicated. Two were forced to flee from Charles County, Maryland. One, named Taylor, was hanged in Dover, Tenn., and two others driven out. One was hanged and another whipped in Cadiz, Ky. One was arrested in Obion, Tenn. The Galveston, Texas, *News* of December 27 reported the frustration of a plot in Houston County and stated, "Arms and ammunition were discovered in several portions of the county, given to them, no doubt, by white men, who are now living among us, and who are constantly inciting our slaves to deeds of violence and bloodshed."

A letter, passed along by whites as well as slaves, found December 24,

1856, on a slave employed on the Richmond and York Railroad in Virginia is interesting from the standpoint of white cooperation and indicates, too, a desire for something more than bare bodily freedom. The letter reads:

> My dear friend: You must certainly remember what I have told you—you must come up to the contract—as we have carried things thus far. Meet at the place where we said, and don't make any disturbance until we meet and don't let any white man know any-thing about it, unless he is trust-worthy. The articles are all right and the country is ours certain. Bring all your friends; tell them, that if they want freedom, to come. Don't let it leak out; if you should get in any difficulty send me word immediately to afford protection. Meet at the crossing and prepare for Sunday night for the neighborhood—
>
> "P.S. Don't let anybody see this—
>
> Freedom—Freeland
Your old friend
W.B.[30]

Another interesting feature of the plots of November and December 1856 is the evidence of the effect of the bitter presidential contest of that year between the Republican, Fremont, and the Democrat, Buchanan. The slaves were certain that the Republican Party stood for their liberation and some felt that Colonel Fremont would aid them, forcibly, in their efforts for freedom. "Certain slaves are so greatly imbued with this fable that I have seen them smile when they were being whipped, and have heard them say that, 'Fremont and his men can hear the blows they receive.'" One unnamed martyr, a slave iron worker in Tennessee, "said that he knew all about the plot, but would die before he would tell. He therefore received 750 lashes, from which he died."[31]

Of the John Brown raid nothing may be said that has not already been told, except that to draw the lesson from the attempt's failure that the slaves were docile, as has so often been done, is absurd. And it would be absurd even if we did not have a record of the bitter struggle of the Negro people against slavery. This is so for two main reasons: first, Brown's raid was made in the northwestern part of Virginia, where slavery was of a domestic, household nature and where slaves were relatively few; secondly, Brown gave the slaves absolutely no foreknowledge of his attempt. The slaves had no way of judging Brown's chances or even his sincerity, and, in that connection, let it be remembered that slave stealing was a common crime in the Old South.

The event aroused tremendous excitement. The immediate result is well described in this paragraph:

> A most terrible panic, in the meantime, seizes not only the village, the vicinity, and all parts of the state, but every slave state in the Union. . . . Rumours of insurrections, apprehensions of invasions, whether well-founded or ill-founded, alters not the proof of the inherent and incurable weakness and insecurity of society, organized upon a slave-holding basis.[32]

Many of these rumors were undoubtedly false or exaggerated both by terror and by anti-"Black Republican" politicians. Bearing this in mind, however, there yet remains good evidence of real and widespread disaffection among the slaves.

Late in November 1859 there were several incendiary fires in the neighborhood of Berryville, Virginia. Two slaves, Jerry and Joe, of Col. Francis McCormick were arrested on the charge of conspiracy and convicted. An effort was made to save these slaves from hanging for it was felt that the evidence against them was not conclusive and that since "We of the South, have boasted that our slaves took no part in the raid upon Virginia, and did not sympathize with Brown,"[33] it would look bad to hang two slaves now for the same crime. Others, however, urged their executions as justified on the evidence and necessary as an example, for "there are other negroes who disserve just as much punishment." The slaves' sentences were commuted to imprisonment, at hard labor, for life.

In December Negroes in Bolivar, Missouri, revolted and attacked their enslavers with sticks and stones. A few whites were injured and at least one slave was killed. Later,

> A mounted company was ranging the woods in search of negroes. The owner of some rebellious slaves was badly wounded, and only saved himself by flight. Several blacks have been severely punished. The greatest excitement prevailed, and every man was armed and prepared for a more serious attack.[34]

Still later advices declared that "the excitement had somewhat subsided."

Early in July 1860 fires swept over and devastated many cities in Northern Texas. Slaves were suspected and arrested.[35] White men were invariably reported as being implicated, and frequent notices of their beatings and executions together with slaves occur. Listing of the counties in which plots were reported, cities burned, and rebels executed will give one an idea of the extensiveness of the trouble and help explain the abject terror it aroused: Anderson, Austin, Dallas, Denton, Ellis, Grimes, Hempstead, Lamar, Milam, Montgomery, Rusk, Tarrant, Walker and Wood. The reign of terror lasted for about eight weeks.

And before it was over reports of disaffection came from other areas. In August a conspiracy among the slaves, again with white accomplices, said to have been inspired by a nearby maroon band, was uncovered and crushed in Talladega County, Ala.[36] About 100 miles south of this, in Pine Level, Montgomery County, of the same state, in that same month, the arrest of a white man, a harness maker, was reported for "holding improper conversations with slaves."[37] Within five months serious difficulty is reported from that region.

Meanwhile, still in August, plots were uncovered in Whitfield, Cobb, and Floyd Counties in Northwest Georgia. Said the Columbus, Ga., *Sun,* of Aug. 29: "By a private letter from Upper Georgia, we learnt that an insurrectionary plot has been discovered among the negroes in the vicinity of Dalton and Marietta and great excitement was occasioned by it, and still prevails." The slaves had intended to burn Dalton, capture a train and crash on into Marietta some seventy miles away. Thirty-six of the slave leaders were imprisoned and the entire area took on a warlike aspect. Again it was felt that "white men instigated the plot," but, since Negro testimony was not acceptable against a white man, the evidence against them was felt to be insufficient for conviction. Another Georgia paper of the same month, the Augusta *Dispatch,* admitting, "we dislike to allude to the evidences of the insurrectionary tendency of things . . . ," nevertheless did deign barely to mention the recent discovery of a plot among the slaves of Floyd County, about forty miles northwest of Marietta.

In September a slave girl betrayed a conspiracy in Winston County, Mississippi. Approximately thirty-five slaves were arrested and yet again it was discovered that whites were involved.[38] At least one slave was hanged as well as one white man described as a photographer named G. Harrington.

Late in October a plot first formed in July was disclosed among the slaves of Norfolk and Princess Anne Counties, Virginia, and Currituck County, North Carolina.[39] Jack and Denson, slaves of a Mr. David Corprew of Princess Anne, were among the leaders. Others were named Leicester, Daniel, Andrew, Jonas and William. These men planned to start the fight for freedom with their spades and axes and grubbing hoes. And it was understood, according to a slave witness, that "white folks were to come in there to help us," but in no way could the slaves be influenced to name their white allies. Banishment, that is, sale and transportation out of the state, was the leaders' punishment.

In November plots were disclosed in Crawford and Habersham

Counties, Georgia.[40] In both places whites were involved. In Crawford a white man, described as a Northern tinsmith, was executed, while a white implicated in Habersham was given five hours to leave. How many slaves were involved is not clear. No executions among them were reported. According to the Southern papers the rebels were merely "severely whipped."

December finds the trouble back again in the heart of Alabama, in Pine Level, Autaugaville, Prattville and Hayneville. A resident of the region declared it involved[41] "many hundred negroes" and that "the instigators of the insurrection were found to be the low-down, or poor, whites of the country." It was discovered that the plot called for the redistribution of the "land, mules, and money." Said another source, the Montgomery, Ala., *Advertiser* of December 13:

> We have found out a deep laid plan among the negroes of our neighborhood, and from what we can find out from our negroes, it is general all over the country. . . . We hear some startling facts. They have gone far enough in the plot to divide our estates, mules, lands, and household furniture.

The crop of martyrs in this particular plot numbered at least twenty-five Negroes and four whites. The names of but two of the whites are known, Rollo and Williamson.

There is evidence of the existence in December 1860 of a widespread secret organization of slaves in South Carolina, dedicated to the objective of freedom. Said J. R. Gilmore, a visitor in the region:

> . . . there exists among the blacks a secret and wide-spread organization of a Masonic character, having its grip, password, and oath. It has various grades of leaders, who are competent and *earnest* men and its ultimate object is FREEDOM.[42]

Gilmore warned a slave leader, Scipio, that such an organization meant mischief. No, said Scipio, "it meant only RIGHT and JUSTICE."

Scipio's parting words were a plea that Gilmore let the North know that the slaves were panting for freedom and that the poor whites, too, were victims of the same vicious system.

* * *

In 1860 there were over 8 million white people in the slaveholding states. Of these but 384,000 were slaveholders among whom were 77,000 owning but one Negro. Less than 200,000 whites throughout the South owned as many as 10 slaves—a minimum necessity for a plantation. And it is to be noted that, while, *in 1850 one out of every three whites was connected, directly or indirectly, with slaveholding, in 1860 only one out of every four had any direct or indirect connection with slaveholding.* Moreover, in certain areas, particularly Delaware, Kentucky, Maryland, Missouri and Virginia, the proportion of slaves to the total population noticeably fell.[43]

These facts are at the root of the maturing class conflict—slaveholder versus non-slaveholder—*which was the outstanding internal political factor in the South in the decade prior to secession.* It is, of course, true generally that, " . . . the real central theme of Southern history seems to have been the maintenance of the planter class in control."[44] But never did that class face greater danger than in the decade preceding the Civil War.

Let us briefly examine the challenges to Bourbon rule in a few Southern states.

In Virginia, at the insistence of the generally free-labor, non-plantation West united with artisans and mechanics of Eastern cities, a constitutional convention was held in 1850–51.[45] On two great questions the Bourbons lost; representation was considerably equalized by the overwhelming vote of 75,748 to 11,063, and the suffrage was extended to include all free white males above twenty-one years of age. The history of Virginia for the next eight years revolves around an ever-sharpening struggle between the slaveholders and non-slaveholders. The power of the latter was illustrated in the election of Letcher over Goggin in 1859 as governor. In that campaign slavocratic rule was the issue and the Eastern, slaveholders' papers appreciated the meaning of Letcher's victory. Thus, for example, the Richmond *Whig* of June 7, 1859, declared:

> Letcher owes his election to the tremendous majority he received in the Northwest Free Soil counties, and in these counties to his anti-slavery record.

In North Carolina, too, there was an "evident tendency of the non-slaveholding West to unite with the non-slaveholding classes of the East,"[46] and this unifying tendency brought important victories. In 1850, for the first time in fifteen years, a Democratic candidate, David S. Reid, captured the governorship, and he won because he urged universal manhood suffrage in elections to the state's senate (ownership of fifty acres of land was then required in order to vote for a senator) as well as to the lower house. Slaveholders' opposition prevented the enactment of such a law for several years but the people never wearied in their efforts and, finally, free suffrage was ratified,[47] August 1857 by a vote of 50,007 to 19,379.

A valiant struggle was also carried on for a more equitable tax system—ad valorem taxation—in North Carolina.[48] A few figures will illustrate the situation. Slaves, from the ages of 12 to 50 only, were taxed 5¾ cents per hundred dollars of their value. But land was taxed 20 cents per hundred dollars, and workers' tools and implements were taxed one dollar per hundred dollars value. Thus, in 1850, slave property worth $203,000,000 paid but $118,330 tax, while land worth $98,000,000 paid over $190,000 in taxes. A Raleigh worker asked in 1860: "Is it no grievance to tax the wages of the laboring man, and not tax the income of their (sic) employer?"

The leader in the fight for equalized taxation was Moses A. Bledsoe, a state senator from Wake County. In 1858 he united with the recently formed Raleigh Workingmen's Association to fight this issue through. He was promptly read out of the Democratic Party, but, in 1860 ran as an independent and was elected. The issue split the Democratic Party in North Carolina and seriously threatened the political strength of the slavocracy. Professor W. K. Boyd has remarked, "one cannot but see in the ad valorem campaign the beginning of a revolt against slavery as a political and economic influence. . . . "[49]

Similar struggles occurred in Texas, Louisiana and South Carolina.[50] In the latter state, for example, the bitter congressional campaign of October 1851 in which secessionists were beaten, again by a united front of farmers and urban workers, by a vote of 25,045 to 17,710, was "marked by denunciations hurled by freemen of the back country against the barons of the low country." The next year a National Democratic Party was launched, led by men like J. L. Orr (later Speaker of the National House), B. F. Perry, and J. J. Evans.[51] Their program cut at the heart of the slavocracy. Let South Carolina abandon its isolationism, let it permit the popular election of the president and governor (both selected by the state legislature), let it end property qualifications for members of its legislature, let it equalize the vicious system of apportionment (which made the slaveholding East dominant), let it establish colleges in the Western part of the state (as it had in the Eastern), and let it provide ample free schools. And, finally, let it enter upon a program of diversified industry. None of these reforms was carried, except partial advance along educational lines, but the threat was considerable and unmistakable.[52]

Overt anti-slavery sentiment was not lacking in the South. This accounts for the fact that, especially in the fifties, scores of white people were driven out of the slaveholding area because of such sentiment in what approached a reign of terror. Another evidence of this has been presented in the material showing that whites were often implicated with slaves in their conspiracies or other efforts at freedom.

The New Orleans *Courier* of October 25, 1850, devoted an editorial to castigating native anti-slavery men, who, it declared, were numerous. Some even thought that two-thirds of the people of New Orleans would be willing to vote for emancipation. An anonymous letter writer said that this was so because there were so many workers in the city who owned no slaves. Earlier that same year a leading Democratic paper of Mississippi, the *Free Trader,* had declared that "the evil, the wrong of slavery, is admitted by every enlightened man in the Union."[53] Professor A. C. Cole has also noted "certain indications which point to a hostility on the part of some of the non-slaveholding Democrats outside of the black belt to the institution of slavery itself."[54]

Competent contemporary witnesses testify to such a feeling, and it certainly was very widespread in Western Kentucky, Eastern Tennessee, Western North Carolina, Western Virginia, and Maryland, Delaware and Missouri.[55]

In order to evaluate properly the effect of the misbehavior of the exploited, Negro and white, upon the mind of the slavocracy, it is instructive to investigate its ideology. Formally, the Democratic Party was derived from Jefferson, but by the 1820s the crux of that democrat's philosophy, *i.e.,* man's right and competence to govern himself, was being scrapped in the South, for one of an authoritarian nature; there has always been slavery, there will always be slavery, and there should always be slavery. And, said the slavocrats, our form of slavery is especially delightful for two reasons: First, our slaves are Negroes, and while slavery is good in itself, the fact that we enslave an "inferior" people makes our slavery particularly good; and, secondly, since ours is not a wage slavery, but chattel slavery, we have no class problem.

Thus Bishop Elliot would declare at Savannah, February 23, 1862, that following the American Revolution,

> . . . we declared war against all authority. . . . The reason of man was exalted to an impious degree and in the face not only of experience, but of the revealed word of God, all men were declared equal, and man was pronounced capable of self-government. . . . Two greater falsehoods could not have been announced, because the one struck at the whole constitution

of civil society as it had ever existed, and because the other denied the fall and corruption of man.[56]

And thus, too, a Georgia paper, the Muskogee *Herald,* of 1856, might exclaim:

> Free society! we sicken at the name. What is it but a conglomeration of greasy mechanics, filthy operatives, small-fisted farmers, and moon-struck theorists?[57]

Again, slaveholders openly bragged—as in an editorial appearing in the *New Orleans Crescent,* October 27, 1859, that the "dragon of democracy, the productive laboring element, having its teeth drawn [is] robbed of its ability to do harm in a state of bondage."

But here were the mechanics and artisans and farmers, Negro and white, of the South, doggedly agitating and conspiring and dying for the same "moon-struck" ideas—liberty and progress! What to do?

There were two ideas as concerns the Negro: reform slavery[58] (legalize marriage, forbid separation of families, allow education); and further repression. The latter, repression, won with hardly a struggle.

The Bourbons were, too, keenly aware of the dangerous trend among the non-slaveholding whites. Propaganda flooded the South to the effect that the interests of slaveholders and non-slaveholders were really the same. Said the press, " . . . arraying the non-slaveholder against the slaveholder . . . is all wrong. . . . The fact that one man owns slaves does not in the least injure the man who owns none."[59]

Slavocracy's leading publicist, J. D. B. DeBow, issued a pamphlet on *The Interest in Slavery of the Southern Non-Slaveholder* (Charleston, 1860), and the politicians played the Bourbons' trump card: the non-slaveholders "may have no pecuniary interest in slavery, but they have a social interest at stake that is worth more to them than all the wealth of the Indies."[60]

But, asked the Bourbons and their apologists, why then does it so often happen that whites aid slaves in their plots? Why, they asked, do some agitate against slavery and distribute "vicious works" like that by North Carolina's "renegade son," Hinton R. Helper's *Impending Crisis* (1857)? Why do they struggle for political and economic reforms similar to those of Northern "moon-struck" theorists?

Merchants and capitalists, even Northern merchants and capitalists, are sympathetic, they reasoned, "but the mechanics, most of them, are pests to society, dangerous among the slave population, and ever ready to form combinations against the interest of the slaveholder, against the laws of the country, and against the peace of the Commonwealth."[61] And "slaves are constantly associating with low white people, who are not slave owners. Such people are dangerous to a community, and should be made to leave our city."[62]

A visitor to Georgia, in December 1859, felt that "the slaveholder seems to watch more carefully to keep the poor white man in subjection than he does to guard the slaves."[63] The North Carolinian Calvin Wiley warned in 1860

> ... that there was as much danger from the prejudice existing between the rich and poor as between master and slave [and felt that] all attempts ... to widen the breach between classes of citizens are just as dangerous as efforts to excite slaves to insurrection.[64]

In 1850 a South Carolinian, J. H. Taylor, had written that:

> ... the great mass of our poor white population begin to understand that they have rights, and that they, too, are entitled to some of the sympathy which falls upon the suffering. ... *It is this great upheaving of our masses we have to fear, so far as our institutions are concerned.*[65]

And in February 1861 another South Carolinian, observing the growth of a white laboring class and its opposition to the slavocratic philosophy declared:

> It is to be feared that even in this State, the purest in its slave condition, democracy may gain a foothold, and that here also the contest for existence may be waged between them.[66]

One month later, March 27, 1861, the Raleigh, N.C., *Register,* observing the increasing class bitterness in its own state, actually "expressed a fear of civil war within the state."[67]

What, then, is the situation? The national supremacy of the slavocracy is gone. And its local power is threatened by both its victims—the slaves and the non-slaveholding whites—separately and, with alarming frequency, jointly. South Carolina Senator James Hammond had warned, in 1847, that slavery's "only hope" was to keep "the actual slaveholders not only predominant, but paramount within its circles."[68]

This "only hope" appeared to be slipping away, if it were not already gone, by 1860. Desperation replaced hope, and desperation—the conviction that there was everything to gain and nothing to lose—led to the slaveholders' rebellion.

And it was *their* rebellion. As one of them, a South Carolinian, A. P. Aldrich, wrote November 25, 1860:

I do not believe the common people understand it; but whoever waited for the common people when a great movement was to be made? We must make the move and force them to follow. That is the way of all great revolutions and all great achievements.[69]

One month later a wealthy North Carolinian, Kenneth Rayner, confided to Judge Thomas Ruffin that he "was mortified to find ... that the people who did not own slaves were swearing that they would not lift a finger to protect rich men's negroes. You may depend on it ... that this feeling prevails to an extent, you do not imagine."[70]

Just a few days before the start of actual warfare Virginia's arch-secessionist, Edmund Ruffin, admitted to his diary, April 2, 1861, that it was

... communicated privately by members of each delegation (to the Confederate Constitutional Convention) that it was supposed people of every State except S. Ca. was indisposed to the disruption of the Union— and that if the question of reconstruction of the former Union was referred to the popular vote, that there was probability of its being approved.[71]

The Raleigh, N. C., *Standard,* whose editor, W. W. Holden, had been read out of the Democratic Party because of his non-slaveholding proclivities, saw very clearly the result of a rebellion whose base was merely several thousand distraught slaveholders. Its editorial of February 5, 1861, warned that

the Negroes will know, too, that the war is waged on their account. They will become restless and turbulent. . . . Strong governments will be established and bear heavily on the masses. The masses will at length rise up and destroy everything in their way. . . .

This article has attempted to present a new emphasis upon a factor hitherto insufficiently appreciated in appraising the causes that drove the slaveholding class to desperation and counter-revolution in 1861. This desperation was not merely due to the growing might of a free-labor industrial bourgeoisie, combined, via investments and transportation ties, with the free West, and to that group's capture of national power in 1860. Another important factor, becoming more and more potent as the slavocracy was being weakened by capitalism in the North, was the sharpening class struggle within the South itself from 1850 to 1860. This struggle manifested itself in serious slave disaffection, in frequent cooperation between poor whites and Negro slaves, and in the rapid maturing of the political consciousness of the non-slavehold-ing whites.

And, taking another step, he who seeks to understand the reasons for the ultimate collapse of the Confederacy will find them not only in the military might of the North, but, in an essential respect, in the highly unpopular character of that government. The Southern masses op-posed the Bourbon regime and it was this opposition, of the poor whites and of the Negro slaves, that contributed largely to its downfall.

Published in *The Communist,* XVIII, February & March, 1939. Reprinted in Herbert Aptheker, *Toward Negro Freedom* (New York: New Century Publishers, 1956), pp 44-67.

On the Centenary of John Brown's Execution

I remember vividly the late Dr. Carter G. Woodson, great pioneer in Negro historiography, telling me that his Harvard history teacher, Professor Edward Channing, admitted he could never think of Old John Brown without an urge to do the man violence, so intense was his hatred for the martyr.

Generally speaking, the hatred among the Learned Ones and the academicians persists; indeed, in the era of the Cold War it has intensified. There are, certainly, some exceptions, and these, being as rare as they are precious, deserve specific notation: Allan Keller, an instructor in journalism at Columbia University, has produced a sympathetic and stirring re-telling of the epic in his *Thunder at Harper's Ferry* (Prentice-Hall, Englewood Cliffs, N. J., 1959), the value of which is enhanced by the splendid reproduction of 32 rare, contemporary illustrations; Oscar Sherwin, a professor of English at City College in New York, in his excellent biography of the great Wendell Phillips, devotes a rich chapter to the Brown drama (*Prophet of Liberty,*

Bookman Associates, N. Y., 1959). Of the greatest value is *A John Brown Reader,* edited, with introduction and commentary by Louis Ruchames (Abelard-Schuman, London & N. Y., 1960). In the introduction, Dr. Ruchames refutes the anti-Brown mythology brewed by James C. Malin and in part poured out again by Professors C. Vann Woodward and Allan Nevins. The body of the book itself consists of articles, letters, memoirs and estimates by and of John Brown—many of these items published here for the first time—which add up to a splendid memorial volume worthy of the great figure here delineated. Still, it is to be noted that these men are not members of history faculties; those sacred precincts remain clear, so far as the published record will show, of any maverick straying from the Channing tradition on John Brown.

Confining ourselves to the past twenty-five years—the present generation—one may offer three representative examples of the conventional treatment of John Brown: Professor Arthur C. Cole, in his *The Irrepressible Conflict,* which was the Civil War volume in the "standard" *History of American Life* edited by A. M. Schlesinger and D. R. Fox—published by Macmillan in 1934—had four words for John Brown: "fanatical abolitionist" and "mad purpose." Professor David Donald, then of Columbia University—now of Princeton—writing in 1948, spared a few more words: "crazy John Brown with a handful of crack-brained disciples" (*Lincoln's Herndon,* Knopf, N. Y.). Professor Michael Kraus, of New York's City College, in a work published in November 1959, characterizes Brown as "fanatical and bordering on the insane" (*The United States to 1865,* a volume in the *University of Michigan History of the Modern World,* edited by Allan Nevins and H. M. Ehrmann, Ann Arbor).

Officials and "leading citizens" of the present town of Harper's Ferry, finding it impossible to give up the chance that the centenary of Brown's attack offered to attract a few additional dollars from tourists, did establish a Harper's Ferry Centennial Association. This Association, according to the *New York Times* (October 4, 1959) set aside four days of events "to commemorate (not 'celebrate,' as one of the officials noted with emphasis) John Brown's raid." The *Times* reporter explained the nice care shown in the choice of verbs, by quoting one of the officials: "John Brown's Raid was embarrassing and untimely when it occurred in 1859, and it apparently still is, today."

One of the featured commemorative events might well have added to the sense of embarrassment. The *Times* reported (Oct. 17, 1959) that "a panel of uncoached (!) experts" discussed John Brown. The uncoached ones included a former editor of the American Legion magazine, three members of the history section of the National Park Service and J. C. Furnas, author of the just-published *Road to Harper's Ferry* (Sloane Associates, N.Y., 1959). The big debate at this discussion revolved around the question of whether or not John Brown was "legally" insane. Mr. Furnas' presence, as well as the auspices, assured that no trace of celebration would enter this centennial commemoration of Brown's effort; his book is so bitter a distillation of the worst said and thought of Brown and the Abolitionist movement that even the *Times* and *Herald-Tribune* reviewers, while praising the book, of course, still felt impelled to enter a slight reservation in terms of Furnas' excessive assaults.

Given such villains, one can guess who are the heroes: *They Who Took Their Stand: The Founders of the Confederacy,* (Putnam, N. Y., 1959), as a new book by Manly W. Welman is called. (There is one noteworthy thing about this book; it manages to display contempt even for John Brown's bravery. For this, one had to wait for a book published in the United States in 1959—the author comments that at his execution, John Brown manifested "animal courage.") Outstanding, of course, in this galaxy of true nobility are Jefferson Davis and Robert E. Lee. Hudson Strode, a well-known novelist, is engaged in producing a three-volume biography of the former. In 1954 he gave us *Jefferson Davis: American Patriot;* in 1959 he brought forth *Jefferson Davis: Confederate President* (Harcourt, Brace, N. Y.); a third—perhaps to be called *Jefferson Davis: Freedom Fighter*—is yet promised us. We suggest the latter as an appropriate finale, since in the second volume, Mr. Strode's central thesis is that Jefferson Davis, "was continually struck by the bitter irony of the North's determination to suppress a proud people, to deny the Southern states their right to freedom according to constitutional pledge." As the reader will observe, Mr. Strode recognizes the ironical when he sees it.

Robert E. Lee, of course, already is apotheosized, his portrait adorning our President's study and one of our country's postage stamps—for all the world like a genuine "freedom fighter." The truly exalted character of General Lee showed itself in the fact that he—a Virginia gentleman, if there ever was one—still felt that chattel slavery was not quite right. And he was so troubled by his doubts that he wrote his wife a letter about it in 1856 admitting that the institution had its dubious features, but noting that for its elimination one had to wait upon the will of God, which was notoriously slow to manifest itself. Indeed, said Lee, to God two thousand years was but a passing day; this the Abolitionists did not understand. The Abolitionists' impatience was contrary to God's way, Lee was sure, and therefore their efforts were dastardly. "Still I fear," continued Lee to his wife, "they will persevere in their evil course. Is it not strange that the descendants of those pilgrim fathers who crossed the Atlantic to preserve their own freedom of opinion, have always proved themselves intolerant of the spiritual liberty of others?"

The one who penned these words—who could easily wait while *others* endured two thousand years of slavery, who saw indubitable evil in those who sought a swifter pace, who took up arms to lead an assault upon his country's flag in order to sever the unity of the Republic (no two thousand years for *that*), and who could see "spiritual liberty" at stake in noninterference with slaveowners—the one who wrote these words is a hero of the Republic whose "moderation" confirms his sanity!

The decisive and the particular feature about John Brown was that he, a white American living in the pre-Civil War era, actually believed, as he often said, that the Negro was the equal of the white and that all men were brothers. John Brown, more than any other pre-twentieth century American white man of record, burned out of himself any sense of white superiority. He, therefore, sought out Negro people, lived among them, listened to them, learned from them—Frederick Douglass, Harriet Tubman, Martin Delany, J. M. Loguen, Dr. and Mrs. J. M. Gloucester, Henry H. Garnet, William Still, Harry Watson, and many more, as well as those who, at Harper's Ferry, pledged their lives to his leadership. Negroes sensed at once, that here was a white man in whom there was no condescension but a real comradeship; they, the most oppressed, and therefore the most sensitive to the needs of justice and the first to recognize sham, loved John Brown as though he were father and brother. It is not possible for an American to earn a greater tribute.

Since John Brown did achieve identification with the Negro people, he felt their enslavement as though it were his own. He dedicated his life, therefore, to contribute to its eradication: "I have only a short time to live—only one death to die," he wrote in 1856. "I will die fighting for this cause."

The first historian, so far as I know, to see and to emphasize this feeling of real brotherhood that Brown achieved, is W. E. B. Du Bois, who wrote, in his splendid interpretive volume, *John Brown* (Philadelphia, 1909): "John Brown worked not simply for the Black Man—he worked with them; and he was a companion of their daily life, knew their faults and virtues, and felt, as few white Americans have felt, the bitter tragedy of their lot."

It is this identification which explains the special hatred felt for Brown among most American academicians and the insistence that the man was mad. In a society where chattel slavery is of fundamental consequence and where its main rationale is the alleged inferiority, if not inhumanity, of the slaves, to strive actively and militantly for the uprooting of that institution and, in doing that, to insist that the institution's rationale is a fraud, naturally provokes the undying hatred of those dominating the institution. Furthermore, the masters of a jim-crow society, having come to terms with the conquered slaveowners and made important assistants out of their lineal descendants, will gladly honor the myths of those assistants and will eagerly incorporate and refine the racist ideology of slavery into the chauvinist ideology of imperialism. Hence, though with some ambiguity and some embarrassment, especially as the "Negro question" takes on a more and more "delicate" character, these masters of jim-crow will honor those the assistants worship and will loathe those the assistants despise.

This is all the more logical in that the Abolitionist assault upon the institution of slavery carried with it—especially amongst the most militant wing of that assault—a questioning of the entire institution of the private ownership of the means of production. Hence the insistence of the most acute of the ideologists of slavery—George Fitzhugh and John C. Calhoun, as examples—that there was no solution to the contradiction involved in class division and no salvation for the rich in the face of the therefore inexorably developing class struggle other than the institution of chattel slavery. Where the workers were so much capital in the pockets of the owners, there and only there was the class struggle exorcised—unless, warned these ideologists, the struggle was to be exorcised through the elimination of the right of ownership; hence, it was urged, all property owners should unite in opposition to the fundamentally seditious tenets of the Abolitionists. This did not occur because there was fundamental antagonism between differing classes of property owners, and because one, the slaveowners, dominated state power and used this to advance their own interests and the others, industrialists, certain merchants, farmers, sought this state power in order to advance their own interests. But when the former was undone, the basis for compromise was already present in the fact that those who emerged victorious were committed to the private ownership of the means of production and would unite with former enemies—or with the devil—if such unity served that fundamental end.

John Brown, having been overpowered by the assault of United States Marines, commanded by Robert E. Lee, with two of his sons dead about him, and with his head bloody from repeated blows with a saber and his body pierced by several bayonet thrusts, was almost at once subjected to an intense grilling by assembled dignitaries and newspapermen. To the baiting and prodding of a reporter from the feverishly pro-slavery *New York Herald,* John Brown said: "You may dispose of me very easily; I am nearly disposed of now; but this question is still to be settled—this Negro question I mean—the end of that is not yet."

And when, under these circumstances, an official demanded to know "Upon what principle do you justify your acts?" Brown replied:

> Upon the golden rule, I pity the poor in bondage that have none to help them; that is why I am here; not to gratify any personal animosity, revenge, or vindictive spirit. It is my sympathy with the oppressed and wronged, that are as good as you and as precious in the sight of God.

With greater development he had made this same point in a long conversation in 1856 with William A. Phillips, covering the Kansas "troubles" for the *New York Tribune.* Phillips recorded:

> One of the most interesting things in his conversation that night, and one that marked him as a theorist, was his treatment of our forms of social and political life. He thought society ought to be reorganized on a less selfish basis; for while material interests gained something by the deification of pure selfishness, men and women lost much by it. He said that all great reforms, like the Christian religion, were based on broad, generous, self-sacrificing principles. He condemned the sale of land as a chattel, and thought there was an infinite number of wrongs to right before society would be what it should be, but that in our country slavery was the "sum of all villanies," and its abolition the first essential work. If the American people did not take courage and end it speedily, human freedom and republican liberty would soon be empty names in these United States.

Brown's sense of class was ever with him and he kept recurring to it. From his prison cell, he wrote a friend on November 1, 1859: "I do not feel conscious of guilt in taking up arms; and had it been in behalf of the rich and the powerful, the intelligent, the great—as men count greatness—of those who form enactments to suit themselves and corrupt others, or some of their friends, that I interfered, suffered, sacrificed, and fell, it would have been doing very well."

It is because this was a thread binding together his whole life, that he enunciated it so clearly and so beautifully when called upon by the Clerk of the Court if he had anything to say before His Honor passed sentence upon him—the clarity and the beauty were present though Brown had not expected to be sentenced at that time and had prepared no written statement; he spoke without notes and without any hesitation. Five paragraphs came from his lips; in one he denied treason, and insisted he did not intend to kill and hence was not guilty of murder; he intended to free slaves and this was his crime. He concluded with remarks absolving all for responsibility in his course, affirmed it was a course imposed upon him by no man and that he himself had imposed his will upon no man who had followed him. But the heart of this immortal "last speech" was in two paragraphs frequently omitted in accounts of what the Old Man said. (For instance, James Ford Rhodes, in the second volume of his *History,* published in 1907, omits these passages; and Michael Kraus, in the book already cited, published in 1959, does the same.) They were, in their entirety, as follows:

I have another objection, and that is that it is unjust that I should suffer such a penalty. Had I interfered in the manner in which I admit, and which I admit has been fairly proved—for which I admire the truthfulness and candor of the greater portion of the witnesses who have testified in this case—had I so interfered in behalf of the rich, the powerful, the intelligent, the so-called great, wife or children, or any of that class, and suffered and sacrificed what I have in this interference, it would have been all right. Every man in this Court would have deemed it an act worthy of reward rather than punishment.

This Court acknowledges, too, as I suppose, the validity of the law of God. I see a book kissed, which I suppose to be the Bible, or at least the New Testament, which teaches me that all things whatsoever I would that men should do to me, I should do even so to them. It teaches me, further, to remember them that are in bonds as bound with them. I endeavored to act up to that instruction. I say I am yet too young to understand that God is any respector of persons. I believe that to have interfered as I have done, as I have always freely admitted I have done, in behalf of His despised poor, I did no wrong, but right. Now, if it is deemed necessary that I should forfeit my life for the furtherance of the ends of justice, and mingle my blood further with the blood of my children and with the blood of millions in this slave country whose rights are disregarded by wicked, cruel, and unjust enactments, I say, let it be done. . . .

It was deemed proper that he so suffer; the Judge, speaking in the name of the State of Virginia, sentenced John Brown to hang by the neck until dead on December 2, 1859, one month after these immortal words were uttered.

John Brown used to the full the six weeks of life left to him from the date of his capture at the Armory until he mounted the scaffold in Charlestown; particularly did he use the month given him from the date of sentence to that of execution. As in the trial he had rejected with scorn and bitterness efforts by court-appointed attorneys to plead insanity for him, so, after being sentenced, he rejected proposals for his rescue coming from Abolitionist friends. The important thing, he had always said, was not to live long, but to live well; now, he added, he was worth infinitely more to the cause of human emancipation at the end of a hangman's noose than he would be as a hunted fugitive.

He conducted himself with such courage and restraint, such consideration and honor that he all but converted his warden to Abolitionism; and that personage together with his guards wept on the day the Old Man was led away to die. Meanwhile, in his interviews and in his steady stream of letters he attacked slavery as an impermissible moral evil and as an institution whose corrosive effect was threatening the existence of the Republic. The reports of these interviews and the texts of these letters were published in the *New York Tribune,* then the newspaper with the largest circulation in the country, and in many other papers and magazines and pamphlets. Public meetings—pro- and anti-Brown—were held in every city and hamlet in the land; what the man said and believed were matters of discussion in every household in the United States. It is probably true that never in the history of the United States had one man's actions and concepts become for so prolonged a period a matter of such intense interest among so vast a proportion of the people as in the case of John Brown.

This is of decisive importance when considering the oft-repeated allegation that the man had "thrown his life away" and that he died as "absurdly" as he had lived. The contrary is the truth. In the life and in the death of John Brown one finds a marvelous merging of the man's meaning; in living and in dying, the Old Man struck powerful blows against the solidity of the "sum of all villanies." As Dr. Du Bois wrote, in the aforementioned book, of "his forty days in prison," Brown, "made the mightiest Abolition document that America has ever known."

Wendell Phillips, addressing a vast mass meeting in Boston on November 18, 1859, taking up this question of "wasted years," said:

> It seems to be that in judging lives, this man, instead of being a failure, has done more to lift the American people, to hurry forward the settlement of a great question, to touch all hearts, to teach us ethics, than a hundred men could have done, living each on to eighty years. Is that a failure?

It may, however, be said that this is self-serving rhetoric, since its author was himself a warm supporter of Brown and had been a militant Abolitionist for over twenty years, and there is force to such an objection. The fact is, however, that on this question, the militant Abolitionists, having most fully identified themselves with the needs of the most oppressed saw therefore most clearly. Here is an instance of the apparent paradox—the achievement of objectivity through the most intense partisanship, so long as that partisanship is with the most oppressed.

Still, in terms of Brown's impact upon the broadest layers of American public opinion, the testimony of Charles Eliot Norton—embodiment of respectability and sobriety—may be more persuasive than that of Phillips. Soon after Brown's execution, this Boston merchant and scholar wrote to an English friend:

> I have seen nothing like it. We get up excitements easily enough . . . but this was different. The heart of the people was fairly reached, and impression has been made upon it which will be permanent and produce results long hence. . . . The events of this last month or two (including under the word events the impression made by Brown's character) have done more to confirm the opposition to slavery at the North than anything which has ever happened before, than all the anti-slavery tracts and novels that ever were written.

John Brown considered the institution of slavery from four points of view: 1) he viewed the Negro people as people, absolutely the equal of all other people, and he therefore considered their enslavement as an abomination; 2) he saw that the institution's continued existence increasingly threatened the freedom and well-being of white Americans and the viability of a democratic Republic; 3) he considered slavery as contrary to the spirit and the letter of the United States Constitution, and therefore as an evil without sound legal warrant; 4) he viewed slavery as institutionalized violence and the slaves as little more than prisoners of war.

In all these views it is possible to affirm—with the hindsight of a century—that John Brown was right, and only on the third point did he stretch matters in terms of historical reality, although even there he grasped more of the truth than those who altogether disagreed with him.

On the fourth point, which led him to the advocacy of militant Abolitionism—i.e., resistance to the violence that was the essence of the slave relationship—there persists considerable disagreement today. Indeed, it is largely because Brown fervently believed this, and then acted on that belief, that he is so widely held to have been mad. Several points are to be considered in this connection. First, the view of slavery which held it to be a state of war between master and slave was classical bourgeois political theory—it is stated quite explicitly, for instance, in the writings of both Montesquieu and Locke, and I have yet to hear either of those two gentlemen called insane. It may be remarked at this point that while both Montesquieu and Locke did so analyze slavery, they did not act toward it in the way that Brown did. That is correct, of course, but to this it may be replied that neither one of them lived in societies characterized and permeated by slavery, so that the stimulus to such action was absent. It may also be replied that because a man carries out in action the logic of his views surely does not prove him insane.

Furthermore, it is a fact that Negro slavery in the United States had its origin in war; it is a fact that its existence was based upon the superior force of the enslaving class and their state apparatus; and it is a fact that its conduct was a constant exercise of coercion and force. Of great importance here was the study which Brown had made of the institution of slavery, especially from this aspect, and his knowledge of the militancy of the Negro slave in direct conflict with the stereotyped views of his alleged passivity and docility. His frequent friendly relationship, in full equality, with many Negro men and women produced in him a clearer view of the realities of American slavery than was vouchsafed to most of his white contemporaries, let alone the moonlight-magnolia-molasses school of mythologists masquerading in the twentieth century as historians.

It is my opinion that with John Brown we are dealing not with madness but with genius. We are dealing with a man who had a profound grasp of the central issues of his era; and with a man of exquisite sensitivity to the needs of his time and of his country. We are dealing, too, with a man whose selflessness was complete.

It is, also, quite impossible to understand Brown rightly if one thinks of him as a man possessed of a view that was unique for his age, and in this sense either fanatical or mentally unbalanced. The fact is that a basic part of Brown's genius was his timing, his knowledge of the mood of the people, and his awareness of how widespread within the Abolitionist movement had become the militant position. [Herbert Aptheker has documented the rise of a militant Abolitionism in his book, *To Be Free* (N. Y., 1948), pp. 41-74.—Editor.]

It is this which explains Brown's enormous impact upon the country; this explains why his act was not dismissed as just the aberrational doings of a lost mind. Brown was sure that he was right; this is why he repeatedly asserted that for him, approaching sixty, it was not so important to live long as it it was to live well. This, too, I think, is why he did not flee from Harper's Ferry when he certainly could have. It is true that he, himself, said that he did not know how to assure the safety of the prisoners he had with him were he to flee, and that this determined him against it until it was too late; surely this was very important. Yet I am bold enough to suggest the other consideration, though I do not know that it ever was explictly asserted by Brown himself.

The noblest souls of his era bowed in grief and tribute when he was hanged. "In teaching us how to die," wrote Thoreau, Brown "at the same time taught us how to live"; Bronson Alcott: "a person of surpassing sense, courage, and religious earnestness"; Louisa May Alcott set down in her diary: "The execution of Saint John the Just took place today"; Emerson, speaking November 8, 1859: "I wish we might have health enough to know virtue when we see it, and not cry with the fools 'madman' when a hero passes." Wendell Phillips, speaking December 8, 1859: "He sleeps in the blessings of the crushed and the poor, and men believe more firmly in virtue, now that such a man has lived." Abroad, Hugo, from his exile, wrote that Brown "was an apostle and a hero; the gibbet has only increased his glory and made him a martyr"; Garibaldi spoke in the same breath of Jesus Christ and John Brown; in Czarist Russia, Brown's martyrdom inspired Chernishevsky.

It was the hanging of John Brown that led James Russell Lowell to create the immortal line: *"Truth forever on the scaffold, Wrong forever on the throne."*

But it was also the temper of the times, that Brown knew so well, that let the poet continue with six words so often omitted but so pregnant with meaning: *"But that scaffold sways the future. . . . "*

It is that same note of defiance and of confidence that was struck by the Negro neighbors of John Brown, who sang as his body was put into the rocky earth of his beloved Adirondacks:

> Blow ye the trumpet, blow
> The gladly solemn sound;
> Let all the nations know,
> To earth's remotest bound,
> The year of jubilee has come.

Two thousand troops, plus cavalry and artillery, surrounded the site of Brown's execution. Seated upon his coffin in the wagon taking him to his death, Brown looked about him and remarked at the beauty of the Blue Ridge. He had already said farewell to his weeping jailers and urged them to regain their composure; he had already handed the immortal note to one of his guards warning that now he knew quite absolutely that much blood would yet have to flow before the cancer of slavery were excised; he had already said his last farewells to his beloved wife (this was the only moment he broke a little, for he wept as she left him); he had already offered cheer to his stalwart and very young comrades waiting their turns into immortality (and each of them, Negro and white, behaved as their leader had taught them to behave). So now was the Old Man driven to the hanging place.

He mounted the gallow steps quickly and firmly. A white hood was placed over his head and his hands were bound behind him. He was led to the trap-door. And then he waited, for all the soldiers had to take their proper stations, and the two thousand seemed more nervous than the sixty-year-old man, bound as he was. An eternity of twelve minutes passed as Brown waited; the executioner asked if he wanted a signal before the trap was sprung, and he said no, thank you, but he would appreciate it if they got on with their work. Did he have anything to say, he was asked; no, he had said all he wanted to say. When all seemed ready, the sheriff called to the executioner himself to do his deadly work and spring the trap, but the man did not hear or did not respond at once, and the call had to be shouted again. At last all was ready and the trap was sprung and the rope (made of cotton, purposely, so that the product of slaves might choke out Brown's life) about his neck sought to strangle its victim. But the Old Man remained alive a full thirteen minutes, while repeated examinations were made of his heart, and finally the physician said he was really dead and he was cut down.

Watching him were Robert E. Lee and the soon-to-be-called "Stonewall" Jackson (who wrote his wife that he feared for Brown's soul) and the actor up from Richmond watching with fascination the fun—the well-known John Wilkes Booth; there, too, among the lines of soldiers was an old man clearly not a soldier whose influence as Virginia's greatest slaveowner and leading theoretician of secession and treason earned him a place—Edmund Ruffin. The latter, four years later, hearing of Lee's surrender to Grant, retired to his study, wrapped his head in the Stars and Bars, put a pistol in his mouth and, belatedly, blew away his mean life.

But less than two years after this hanging, an army of two million was crushing the life out of slavery and treason, inspired in their work by *"John Brown's body lies amouldering in the ground, but his soul goes marching on."* And about three years later, the great Frederick Douglass was conferring in the White House with the President of the United States (for the first time in history a Negro found himself in this position). And the president was asking the Negro statesman how best the government might get the news of the Emancipation Proclamation into the heart of the South so that the slaves might learn of it and act upon its news and so cripple the might of the Confederacy. Frederick Douglass tells us:

> I listened with the deepest interest and profoundest satisfaction, and at his suggestion, agreed to undertake the organizing of a band of scouts, composed of colored men, whose business should be, somewhat after the original plan of John Brown, to go into the rebel states beyond the line of our armies, carry the news of emancipation, and urge the slaves to come within our boundaries.

Surely here is a neatness to historical vindication that has few equals!

On December 2, 1859, memorial services were held for John Brown at the Town Hall of Concord, Massachusetts, where revolutionists had fired the "shot heard around the world." Edmond Sears, the pastor of the nearby village of Wayland, wrote and read these lines upon that occasion:

> Not any spot six feet by two
>   Will hold a man like thee;
> John Brown will tramp the shaking earth
>   From Blue Ridge to the sea,
> Till the strong angel comes at last
>   And opes each dungeon door,
> And God's Great Charter holds and waves
>   O'er all his humble poor.

And then the humble poor will come
In that far-distant day,
And from the felon's nameless grave
They'll brush the leaves away;
And gray old men will point this spot
Beneath the pine-tree shade,
As children ask with streaming eyes
Where old John Brown is laid.

From Concord grounds to Charlestown gallows is a straight line; and the Americans who perished there brought nearer "the far-distant day." There is no higher patriotism than to so live that having died men may say: "He gave his whole life to hastening that day." This is the heritage for all mankind bequeathed by the American Martyr, John Brown, and this is the measure of the man's greatness.

Published in *Political Affairs,* XXXVIII, December 1959, pp. 13-25. Reprinted as a pamphlet, *John Brown: American Martyr* (New York: New Century Publishers, 1960).

3
SAVING THE REPUBLIC

The Civil War

In its origin, the Civil War in the United States was an attempted counterrevolution carried out by a desperate slaveholding class. The aggressors were the dominant elements among the slaveowners, and the resort to violence was long planned, carefully prepared and ruthlessly launched. There was not unanimity among the slaveowners; some feared that the resort to violence would fail and that its result would be the destruction of the slave system. But those who so argued were overruled and the richest and most powerful among the planter-slaveholders carried the day for secession and war.

Why did the slaveholding class violently attack the government of the United States in 1861? It did so because it had become convinced that it had everything to gain and nothing to lose by a resort to violence; and, in the past, whenever an exploitative ruling class has reached this decision—*and had the power to do so*—it turned to violence. Here, specifically, the decisive elements in the slaveholding oligarchy came to the conclusion that if they acquiesced in the developments culminating in Lincoln's election in 1860, they would, in fact, acquiesce in their own demise; that if, on the contrary, they did not passively yield, but refused to accept this culmination, they had, at any rate, a fighting chance to reverse the course of those developments. In other words, they decided: If we yield now we shall be buried; if we do not, we may win and so bury another. But if we lose we shall be no worse off than if we did not fight—i.e., if we lose we shall then be buried. Given belief in such an alternative—and given the capacity to undertake it and carry it out—all exploitative ruling classes have chosen the path of counter-revolutionary violence. Such classes are devoid of humanistic feelings; suffering means nothing to them, since their rule is posited on human travail and their wealth and power derive from its infliction; such considerations were especially marked among the American slaveowners—arrogant, ruthless and racist to the core.

Affirming that a sense of desperation drove the slaveholding class onto the path of counterrevolutionary violence, leads at once to the question: what made this class desperate? What convinced its leaders that they had everything to gain and nothing to lose if they chose the path of civil war?

There were four great forces producing this result, interpenetrating and influencing each other.

First: the momentous socio-economic transformation of the United States north of the Mason-Dixon line and extending from the Atlantic Ocean to the Mississippi River; second: the quantitative and qualitative growth of the Abolitionist movement; third: the intensification of mass unrest and class conflict within the South; fourth: the accumulating impact of certain organic contradictions within the plantation-slavery system.

The basic nature of the shift in socio-economic foundations in the North appearing with the Revolutionary War, accelerating with the War of 1812 and its aftermath and accumulating speed after 1840—was the growing weight of industrialization and urbanization. It is in the decade of 1850–1860 that the value of the product of the factories approaches the value of the product of the soil for the first time in American history; that is the great water-shed mark. Before that, agriculture had significantly outweighed industry in the total economy; after that the reverse was to be increasingly true. The turning point comes in the decade preceding secession and marking the appearance and growth of the new Republican Party. In 1790 about 5% of the total population was urban (living in places of 2,500 inhabitants or more); in 1830 about 8% was urban; in 1860 about 20% was urban—and while this urbanization did not completely skip the South, it was overwhelmingly concentrated in the North.

The population leap in the United States is remarkable in the pre-

Civil War generation, rising from 12.8 million in 1830 to 31.4 million in 1860, but while half the population of the country lived in the South in 1830, about one-third the population of the country lived there in 1860. In the 1830s immigration to the United States averaged about 50,000 per year; in the 1850s immigration averaged about 250,000 each year—and the vast majority of these newly-arrived working people settled outside the slave-ridden areas.

A rising industrial bourgeoisie was one of the results of these developments; but the predominant class in the government of the United States in the 1830s and 1840s was the slaveholding class. Its predominance was not without challenge, and increasing challenges, as the years passed and the changes accumulated, but that class did rule. It dominated Congress and its committees; it dominated the presidency; it had a majority in the Supreme Court; apologia for slavery characterized the prevailing and respectable institutions—the press, the churches, the schools, the texts. A domestic and foreign policy to the liking of the slaveholding class characterized U. S. history during these decades. This politico-ideological superstructure became increasingly anachronistic and inhibiting as the socio-economic base was transformed in the manner indicated. Hence, political and ideological battles and recurring crises marked the period from the late 1840s and especially the 1850s; the culmination, politically, was the smashing of the two-party system, the emergence of a new, broad, coalition-type party, under the hegemony of the industrial bourgeoisie, and the ultimate victory of that party in the 1860 elections.

Additional decisive changes were occurring in the socio-economic structure of the North. With the rise of industry and with urbanization, appeared a more and more numerous working class, and both its organization and its consciousness intensified as the Civil War approached. They found the institution of slavery more and more reprehensible—here the influx of thousands of revolutionary exiles from the Europe of 1830 and 1848 played a significant role—and found their own interests less and less considered insofar as the federal government and its policies were concerned, dominated as that government was by the slaveowners. Fundamental ideological conflict appeared, especially as the challenged and distraught slavocracy began to develop a full-blown theory of the propriety and necessity—if "civilization" were to survive—of the enslavement of the laboring portion of any country's population, whether its complexion be light or dark.

Significant distinctions began to appear among the commercial bourgeoisie of the North. With the growth of factories in the North and the development of agricultural production there, slave-grown produce played a smaller and smaller part in the businesses of Northern merchants. Increasingly, these merchants were engaged in hauling and selling corn, wheat, cattle-products, machinery, shoes, clothing, furniture, rather than sugar, tobacco, rice and cotton. The merchant bourgeoisie had been the fundamental political allies of the slaveholding planters and the bulwark of the northern wing of the Democratic Party, generally the preferred party of those planters. Now, this Northern economic and political bulwark was split; this is of basic importance in comprehending the actual division that occurred in the Democratic Party with the election of 1860, so that two Democratic Party candidates ran for the Presidency (Douglas of Illinois on the Northern ticket and Breckinridge of Kentucky on the Southern)—without which split, Lincoln would not have been successful.

Meanwhile what was then the West—from the Ohio to the Mississippi to the Great Lakes—was being swiftly populated. Pressure mounted for a rapid and democratic land-settlement policy on the part of the Federal government, only to meet the rigid resistance of the planters; at the same time, the movement was made possible because of the tying together of the East and the West with thousands of miles of newly-laid railroads. This in turn fed the growth of industry in the northeast; it served, also, to unite the farm west and the factory east, and to defeat Calhoun's grand plan of an agricultural united front of western farmers and southern planters and farmers which would outweigh the urbanizing east.

This socio-economic transformation showed itself, among other aspects, in the smashing of the traditional political apparatus, and in the coming to the fore, through the new party, of new demands appropriate to the interests of the developing classes: a protective tariff, internal improvements at federal expense, national currency and banking legislation, a homestead law, the exclusion of slavery from the federal lands, a reversal of domestic and foreign policies favoring the slaveholders, including the rejection of the vitiating of the Bill of Rights which had been so prominent a part of the cost of maintaining slavery.

Unless one sees the revolutionary nature of the Abolitionist movement, he cannot understand it. This movement hitherto has been presented as either the unfortunate fruit of the labors of mischievous fanatics or as some kind of liberalistic, reformistic, benevolent enterprise. These views agree in ignoring the fundamental character of the movement: a Negro-white, radical effort to revolutionize America, by overthrowing its dominant class. That is, Abolitionism sought the elimination of that form of property ownership which was basic to the power of the slaveholding class, and it was that class which effectively dominated the government of the United States during the pre-Civil War generation.

The movement, being revolutionary, suffered persecution and fierce denunciation; but its members—Negro and white, men and women, Northerners and Southerners, with a large percentage of youth, and almost all of them not of the rich—persevered, as true revolutionaries, and finally led the nation to victory. Its great curse, early in its life was sectarianism; it advocated courses which persistently narrowed its appeal—for instance, an extreme pacifism and anarchism. But as the classes objectively opposed to the continued domination of slavery grew, as the existence of slavery in the United States became a more and more intolerable stench in the nostrils of civilized peoples in the world, as the struggles of the slaves themselves mounted, and as the reactionary offensive of the slaveowners impinged on the rights and beliefs of ever wider elements in the population, the movement itself grew. As it grew it found the sectarianism more and more contradictory and absurd and so developed a much more rounded, flexible and politically astute outlook; this in turn stimulated further growth. This growth was qualitative as well as quantitative; the movement turned more and more to effective political efforts and to the renunciation of a crippling kind of pacifism, especially in the face of the institutionalized violence of the slaveowners.

Increasingly, as the 1840s gave way to the 1850s, the Abolitionists became admired and respected leaders of groups decisive in both an ideological and a political sense; by the 1850s the *New York Tribune*—the newspaper with the largest circulation in the nation, whose European correspondent was Karl Marx—was decidedly anti-slavery, though not actually Abolitionist.

It is not without interest that some of this sectarianism infected working-class oriented and even Marxist-inspired groups. Some tended to view the conflict between a slave-based agrarianism and a wage-labor based industrialism as merely a contest between two sets of "bosses" concerning which "real" Marxists could have no choice.

Fortunately, Marx was then very much alive and when he was appealed to for his opinion as to whether or not Marxian socialists should take a "plague-on-both-your-houses" position in this conflict, he replied that he was appalled that anyone alleging adherence to his views could possibly raise such a question. Of course, Marx insisted, socialists were the strongest foes of chattel slavery because, in the first place, they desired the liberation of four million slaves and because, in the second place, as between industrial capitalism and agrarian slaveholding, the former was the more progressive force and the latter was completely backward and regressive.

The quantitative and qualitative growth of the Abolitionist movement was seen by the slave-owning class. Its culmination in the sensational success of *Uncle Tom's Cabin* early in the 1850s, the extraordinary sale and influence of the economic analysis of the backwardness of slavery produced by Hinton Rowan Helper, a non-slaveholder from North Carolina, under the title *The Impending Crisis* (1857), and then the noble martyrdom of immortal John Brown and his Negro and white comrades, and the intense sympathy they aroused throughout the North and the world, helped create a sense of panic and desperation in the minds of the dominant slaveowners.

The rulers of the South always have sought to propagate the idea that their region is "solid," is united in support of the "way of life" characterizing the area. This effort is made today, and the picture it seeks to spread is quite false; the effort was made in the days of slavery, and the picture conventionally presented of that epoch—of a monolithic South with the Negro slaves cherishing their chains and with all the whites, regardless of class position, firmly committed to slaveholding dominance in the name of white supremacy—also was thoroughly false.

The fact is that the slave South was an area torn by antagonism and basic contradictions: slaves versus slaveowners, large slaveowners versus the smaller slaveowners, the non-slaveholding whites versus the slaveholding whites, and especially opposed to the richest among them. Far from the Negro people being docile and "ideal" slaves, they created a heritage of militant and ingenious struggle during their crucifixion that has no superior among any people on earth. They resisted their oppressors in every possible way: they "slowed up" in their work; they fled by the thousands; they rose individually in rebellion; they plotted and rebelled collectively scores of times; they infused their stories and songs and music and religion—every aspect of their lives—with this central theme: resist slavery; struggle for freedom. In this sense the magnificent liberation struggles of the American Negro people today are in direct line with and represent a splendid continuation of the profoundest traditions of their entire history.

This militancy reached its highest point, in the history of American slavery, during the decade from 1850 through 1860. In that period more slaves fled—singly and in groups—than ever before; more individual assaults against slaveowners occurred than ever before; more slave conspiracies and uprisings occurred than before, and many of them had a deeper political content—including the demands for the distribution of the land—than before, and characteristically in this decade, unlike the previous period, whites were involved in such plots and uprisings. The master class was keenly aware of this intensified unrest of the slaves; their private letters, diaries and newspapers are filled with concern about it.

Class struggle between slaveowners and non-slaveowners characterizes all Southern politics from about 1790 on; but this reached its most intense and most widespread form in the years from 1850 to 1860. The struggle appeared in the growing cities and especially in the predominant agrarian areas. It took the form of the creation of new antislaveowners political parties, and of significant organized efforts by the non-slaveowners to overthrow the political domination of the plantation lords. The aim was the remaking of the political structure, of the taxation system, of the educational system; the aim was the achievement of something approximating an advanced bourgeois-democratic society. Its greatest weakness was that while it opposed the slaveowning class, it did not oppose slavery as such; while it hated the planters, it lost no love for the slaves. The whole system of chattel slavery made extremely difficult the forging of unity among the Negro and white victims of the plantation oligarchy, and while some advances towards such unity were made—and terrified the Bourbons—the fact is that these advances fell far short of the achievement of any real solidarity.

But, while the effort to overthrow the dominance of the slaveholding oligarchy within the South was not successful, it was serious and it worried that oligarchy very much. Many of its leaders actually feared civil war at home before they could launch their counterrevolutionary effort against Washington. This internal challenge to the continued domination of the South by the Bourbons has been relatively neglected in the literature; it is, nevertheless, one of the fundamental forces driving the slaveholding class to the desperate strategy of creating the Confederacy and attacking the United States government.

In addition to the forces already described, certain contradictions organic to the nature of the plantation system, as a socio-economic system, were plaguing it and driving its masters distraught. First, the system was one that required steady and swift expansion in order to live. The system existed for the purpose of realizing a profit from the sale of commodities in a world market. The rate of profit rose in direct correlation with the increase in the number of slaves employed and in the acreage tilled, especially the tilling of virginal lands, where the crops per acre rose. The system of slavery, where mechanization was minimized and scientific farming was almost unknown, required constant expansion. Here fertilization, dry-farming, varying the crops planted, etc., either was not comprehended or was not practical, or the necessary fluid capital was not at hand—especially in view of the fact that about one thousand dollars of capital was tied up in the ownership of each slave.

The system of American slavery was intensely oligarchic; it moved rather quickly towards the declassing of the smaller slaveowners and the concentration of the ownership of slaves and more and more land— and the best land—in the hands of fewer and fewer great planters. While 35 percent of the white population in the South had some interest— direct or indirect, through family—in slaveholding in 1850, this figure had dropped to 25 percent by 1860. It is this sharp oligarchic tendency in the slave system which accounts for the intensity of the class struggle characterizing it; and it is the especially swift rate of such concentration during the pre-Civil War decade that explains the particularly sharp nature of the class struggle marking that period.

The natural tendency towards expansionism of the slave system had two other significant stimulators. One was the fact that the piling up of a slave population within a restricted area intensifies police problems. Such problems were considerable in any case; they might reach Santo-Domingo proportions, with equally disastrous results for the slaveholders, if they did not manage to acquire new land regularly into which the slave population could be sent and thus that "dangerous" component in the population diffused.

In addition, plantation expansionism had a clear political motive. Slavery in the United States—localized in the South—faced the development of the free-labor system outside of the South. One of the meeting places of this developing conflict was the federal public lands; if these were to be settled by free farmers and workers and by a wage-based bourgeoisie then the political weight of the West would fall on the anti-slavery side and the planters' domination of the federal government would end.

For all these reasons, the expansionism of the slave-South was intense and notorious. It helped precipitate war with Mexico in the 1840s—a rather unpopular war outside the South; it helped account for filibustering assaults against Nicaragua a little later; for the diplomatic pronouncement by three U. S. Ministers in Europe that Cuba should belong to the United States and not to Spain; and for the naval expedition financed by the U. S. government through the Amazon Valley region of Brazil, with an eye to weighing its possibilities as a base for an extended slave empire.

At the same time, this expansionism precipitated the sharpest kinds of political struggles on the national election scene; it was the Republican Party's promise that "not a foot" of federal soil would be given over to slavery—and Lincoln's insistence, after his election, on keeping that promise—that finally decided the slaveowners that whatever the Republican Party might promise as to the sanctity of slavery "where it was," the promise was useless in fact since if slavery could not expand into where it was not, it could not last long where it was.

The Confederate assault upon Washington and the secession from the United States was a counterrevolutionary development. It was counterrevolutionary not only in its regressive motivations and its profoundly anti-democratic essence—challenging as it did the integrity of the bourgeois-democratic republic and the ideology of the Declaration of Independence; it was counterrevolutionary, too, in that it was done secretly, with malice aforethought, and *against the will of the vast majority of the Southern people.* One-third of those people—the Negro masses—abhorred the Confederacy, of course, and desired nothing so much as its destruction which, they knew, would mean their own emancipation. But, in addition, the majority of the eight million Southern white people—there were in 1860 only about 300,000 actual slaveowners—also detested the planting oligarchy and also were opposed to secession and to the whole Confederate conspiracy.

The bulk of the literature on the Civil War assumes or asserts the contrary, and insists that the Confederate movement had the overwhelming support of the masses of Southern whites, at least. But the truth is the opposite. This is why the leaders of secession made no effort to submit the question of secession to a vote of the restricted electorate in the Southern states—prior to secession—and why, in fact, they resisted all proposals for such a vote. It is for this reason, too, that this so-called popular uprising disintegrated when put to the test of a war carried to the South by the invading and—allegedly—bitterly despised foe.

In eight states of the Confederacy the question of secession was never submitted to a vote of the electorate. In the three states where the question of secession was voted upon—Virginia, Tennessee, and Texas—this was not done until after each of them had already been committed to the Confederacy, and hostilities had actually begun (except for Texas, where the voting occurred on Feb. 25, 1861). Further-more, even the voting—held under war-time conditions, with secession an accomplished fact, and with secessionists counting the votes—showed these results: Texas, for secession, 34,794; against, 11,235; Virginia, for secession, 128,884; against, 32,134; Tennessee, for seces-sion, 104,019; against, 47,238. Moreover, even in these three, Tennessee split in half, Virginia split in half, and the governor of Texas (the anti-secessionist, Sam Houston) was illegally superseded.

Only this background makes understandable the complete disin-tegration of the Confederacy when it was put to the test of battle. Pro-Bourbon historians, faced with this utter collapse, have no real explanations. Thus, for example, Professor E. Merton Coulter, co-editor of the multi-volumed and "definitive" *History of the South,* in the volume which he himself wrote in that series, *The Confederate States of America* (1950), "explains" the collapse by saying it resulted from a "loss of morale," that "the spirit of the people gave way" (p. 70); or, "why did the Confederacy fail? . . . The people did not will hard enough and long enough to win" (p. 566).

But Coulter's explanation explains nothing; it rather poses the question in different words. Why was there a "loss of morale"; why did "the spirit of the people give way"? Because it was not a popular war; because Congressman Aldrich and Governor Richardson and Edmund Ruffin, and the members of the Confederate Constitutional Conven-tion were correct when they feared that the Southern white people—let alone the Negroes—did not favor secession.

Nowhere was Karl Marx's genius more dramatically demonstrated than in his grasp of the real nature of the Civil War and in his comprehension of the unpopular character of the Confederacy. The military experts of the world were agreed that the North would not be able to defeat the South; at best they saw a long and drawn-out war exhausting both sides with some kind of military draw resulting and a negotiated settlement concluding the conflict. Marx disagreed; he held that the North would defeat the South and do so rather quickly and accomplish it utterly. And Marx insisted on this exactly because he knew it was not the North versus the South, but rather the United States versus a slaveholding oligarchy. Marx, of course, paid careful attention to the class forces involved in the struggle; he followed with close attention the procedure of secession; he noted that no plebiscite on this was permitted. He insisted upon the oligarchic and non-popular character of the Confederacy.

The world's military profession agreed that the Confederacy, with its great population, its enormous area, its tremendous coastline, its numerous military cadre, would never be defeated by the North (this was another reason for the failure of France and England to intervene more actively than they did on the side of the Confederacy—why do so when she *could* not lose?) Indeed, even Frederick Engels seriously doubted the outcome of the war, and as late as September 1862, asked Marx: "Do you still believe that the gentlemen in the North will crush the 'rebellion'?"

Marx replied that he "would wager his head" on that belief. It was based, he wrote, not only on Lincoln's supremacy in resources and men (for this alone need not be decisive—witness the American colonies versus Great Britain, Holland versus Spain, etc.), but also on the fact that the South was not in rebellion, but that rather an oligarchy of some 300,000 slaveholders had engineered a counterrevolutionary *coup d'etat.*

Individual monographic studies by Laura White, Georgia L. Tatum, Olive Stone, Herbert Aptheker, Albert Moore, Charles Wesley, John K. Bettersworth, Harvey Wish, Roger W. Shugg, W. E. B. Du Bois, Bell Wiley, and others have demonstrated the enormous amount of popular disaffection—among Negro and white—which bedeviled the Confederacy, ranging from mass desertions, organized guerrilla warfare (of which, by the way, there was almost none inside the South *against the Union forces),* mass flights of slaves, strikes in factories, hunger demonstrations and riots, anti-conscription outbreaks, etc.

When one remembers the degree of treason among the officer caste in

the United States Army—with almost none among the enlisted men—
the pro-Confederate activities of Buchanan's Administration in the
days before Lincoln took office, the Copperheadism in the North, the
white chauvinism there, the graft and corruption with which the
bourgeoisie always conducts government and especially government
faced with war, the hostility of most Western European governments to
Abraham Lincoln's government and the assistance given the Confederacy, one must conclude that there were grounds, apparently, for
the belief that the North would lose. In the face of all these sources of
weakness, Lincoln's victory—and within four years, little enough time,
as nineteenth century wars were conducted, especially in the vast
distances of the United States—could not have transpired without the
active opposition to the Confederacy by the overwhelming majority of
Southern people.

In the result of the War, the sympathy for the cause of the Union felt
by the common people of all Europe, of Canada and of Mexico was
important. The role of the First International, under the personal
leadership of Karl Marx, in helping to organize and focus this popular
opposition, especially in Great Britain, is well-known. Less well known
is the important contribution to the Union cause made by the Mexican
revolutionary masses, led by the great Benito Juarez, in resisting the
efforts of France to conquer Mexico. Had this conquest been complete
and not seriously contested, the Confederacy would have had a long
land border with a friendly French power, and this would have added
difficulties to the imposition of an effective blockade of the Confederacy. It is somewhat ironic that the Mexican masses helped preserve the integrity of the United States, less than twenty years after the
United States had stolen from Mexico, through war, one-third of its
own territory.

In the actual fighting of the war, it was the common people—the
working men and the farming masses—who bore the brunt of the
battle, made the sacrifices in blood, crushed the Confederacy, and
saved the American Republic. The basic patriotism of these masses—in
the South and in the North—came to the fore and with it grew an
understanding of the stakes of the conflict so far as the cause of
democracy was concerned.

By now a considerable literature depicting in truthful and realistic
terms the absolutely decisive role of the Negro people in the Civil War
has made its appearance. It was to maintain and extend the system of

their enslavement that the counterrevolution was launched; here one has a classical example of the profound involvement of the general fate of the United States, and especially of the democratic advancement of the United States, with the specific condition of the Negro people. Here one sees how the system of the Negro's special oppression almost caused the suicide of the entire American republic.

The Negro leadership was in the forefront of the effort to make clear the decisive nature of the slave system to the power of the Confederacy; it therefore led in advancing the necessity to revolutionize the conduct of the war. The war, if conducted passively, defensively, if conducted only to "defend the Union" with an insistence that the institution of slavery was irrelevant to the conflict, would not terminate happily for the Union. No, to defend the Union it was necessary to destroy the power base of those who attacked it; to defend the Union it was necessary to add to its resources the mighty power and passion of the Negro millions. To defend the Union it was necessary to destroy slavery. The salvation of the Union required the emancipation of the slaves; the emancipation of the slaves required the salvation of the Union. Thus did the dialectics of history manifest itself in specific form in the great Civil War.

The process of revolutionizing the conduct of the war was a relatively prolonged one; and it was one that required agitation, organization and struggle. In this, the Negro masses were in the front ranks. And when success was achieved in the basic change of strategy, to implement the change, the Negro fighter would have to step forward and show his mettle. The Negro people did so and did so with decisive results for the course of the war. About 220,000 Negro men fought as soldiers; about 25,000 battled as seamen. Another 250,000 Negro men and women served Lincoln's forces as teamsters, scouts, pioneers (what are now called engineer troops), cooks, nurses, fortification and railroad builders, etc. And, in the South, the Negro masses were the eyes and ears of the advancing Union forces; without effective military intelligence, battles and wars cannot be won. The best source of such intelligence for Lincoln's army and navy came from the Negro masses who knew—and know—the South better than anyone else. Meanwhile, Negro slaves fled by the thousands—probably half a million succeeded in fleeing during the four years of war—and in doing this withdrew their labor power from the despised Confederacy and brought it to the side of the Union. Dr. Du Bois once characterized this phenomenon of mass flight as a kind of "mobile general strike" and the observation is highly illuminating.

Conventional American historiography—deeply chauvinist as it is—presents the Civil War as a white man's quarrel as a result of which rather absent-mindedly the Negro people were *given* their freedom. Nothing could be further from the truth; the basic connection between the institution of slavery and the source and nature of the Civil War is clear, and the active role of the Negro people in fighting for their own emancipation—and for the integrity of the Republic—is established by the evidence. Rather than declaring that the American Negro people were given their freedom as an incident of the War for the Union, it would be more accurate to say that the Negro people contributed decisively towards the salvation of the Union as part of their heroic battle to achieve emancipation.

This whole matter shows again the deep interpenetration of the history and struggles of the Negro people with the struggles of the mass of the American people altogether to advance the cause of progress and democracy; it shows, too, that in this organic connection no one is doing anyone else any favors. This matter of Negro-white unity is a question not of benevolence but of alliance.

Policies of compromise and gradualism—both of which were advocated and followed prior to, and even during the early phases of the war—are disastrous. Especially where the Negro question is concerned—this being a principled question—such policies reflect in fact acquiescence in Negro oppression; they are devices not for the elimination of such oppression, but for its continuation.

The Civil War demonstrates that decisive governmental acts are of the greatest importance where the fight for Negro liberation is concerned. Such acts possess tremendous practical and educational significance. Thus, it was widely held that it was "impossible" to make soldiers of Negro men, give them guns and put them in the field fighting with white men against other white men. But what was held to be "impossible" was soon seen not only to be possible, but necessary. Since its necessity was comprehended by the Lincoln government—with that government being prodded by the Negro people and the Abolitionists in general—it did adopt the policy of arming Negro men and putting them into combat on land and in the sea. And there was nothing "impossible" about it; the dire prophecies as to what would happen and how whole regiments of white soldiers would desert at once, etc., did not come to pass.

They did not come to pass because the Lincoln government made it clear that it was serious about this policy and because that government said that its own existence depended upon the enforcement of that policy.

Similar results—after the expression of similar fears—followed other Executive acts, such as the recognition of the Negro Republic of Haiti, the equalization of pay between Negro and white soldiers, and—decisive act that it was—the issuance of the Emancipation Proclamation.

The basic structure of modern America is laid down with the Civil War and its outcome. The unity of the republic is confirmed; the preservation of the bourgeois-democratic form is achieved. Industrial capitalism emerges triumphant and dominant; it fastens its grip upon the State and it leaps forward mightily as an economic force. Organization of this bourgeoisie on a national scale is achieved and it moves swiftly ahead toward achieving complete hegemony over the national market. At the same time, with the leap ahead of industrial capitalism, its necessary antagonist leaps forward too; the working class multiplies in a short period and becomes very much more highly organized—also upon a national scale—by 1866 than it had been in 1860.

By constitutional amendments—the Thirteenth and Fourteenth—the institution of chattel slavery is prohibited and efforts at compensation by some of the former slaveowners thwarted. Here appeared an extremely significant precedent; these amendments consummated a revolutionary transformation. With the Thirteenth Amendment, several billion dollars worth of private property—hitherto perfectly legal—were confiscated and by this blow a basic element in an entire social fabric was eliminated. This was done on the basis of the reactionary and truly subversive character of such property ownership; it is a revolutionary precedent that the present ruling class prefers should be forgotten.

In preserving the bourgeois democratic form, in the leap forward of industrial capitalism, in its achieving governmental domination, in the destruction of the system of chattel slavery, in the emancipation of four million Negro men and women, in the advance of the labor movement, the American Civil War, which begins as a counterrevolutionary effort, terminates as the Second American Revolution.

That the industrial bourgeoisie, swiftly moving towards monopoly status, coveting the enormous resources of the South, desiring the retention in the country of a large mass of especially exploited working people, and wanting the political support of the former slaveowners, fail to complete this Revolution is another question. They are a leading element in the coalition of forces which hurls back the threat of the slaveowners, but when that common foe is defeated, the bourgeoisie betrays the coalition—and especially the Negro people. It allows the former slaveowners to remain the dominant plantation owners; it makes of them satraps—"little foxes," in the words of Lillian Hellman's incisive drama—and the basis of the Republican-Dixiecrat reactionary alliance is laid back in the 1870s betrayal of the hopes of the masses.

Much unfinished business remains from the Civil War, and much more unfinished business has accumulated for the forces of democracy and peace in the century since that war was fought. The "handling" of these questions creates every day's headlines in the American press; they remain fundamental social questions, on a new level, for the United States of the 1960s.

Their nature cannot be understood, however, without a comprehension of the great struggle waged in the United States from 1861 to 1865. That struggle was a momentous landmark in the effort to secure a "government of the people, by the people, for the people." The struggle continues, on new and higher levels, in our time. The American people have not been found wanting in the decisive struggles of the past, and they will not be found wanting in our own new and challenging epoch.

Published as a pamphlet, *The American Civil War* (New York: International Publishers, 1961).

The Emancipation Proclamation

Contemporaries differed most sharply in their reactions to Lincoln's Emancipation Proclamation, issued in preliminary form on September 22, 1862, and in final form on January 1, 1863. The differences reflected the class divisions in the United States and demonstrated the truth that ideas basically derive from the groundwork of these divisions.

Much of the Northern press, especially that controlled by merchants with close ties to slaveowners, as the *New York Herald* and the *Journal of Commerce,* denounced the Proclamation. Many of the reactions were so vehement that the President, reading, as he said, "a batch of editorials," was moved to ask himself: "Abraham Lincoln, are you a man or a dog?"

The Confederate press, as one would expect, spewed vitriol rather than ink. The *Richmond Enquirer,* for example, asked with reference to the President and his Proclamation: "What shall we call him? Coward, assassin, savage, murderer of women and babies? Or shall we consider them all as embodied in the word fiend, and call him Lincoln, the Fiend?"

Copperheadism in the North matched the elevated language of its Southern ideological brethren, so that, as an instance, the Democratic-dominated legislature of Lincoln's own Illinois formally resolved that his Proclamation was "a gigantic usurpation . . . a total subversion of the Federal Union . . . an uneffaceable disgrace to the American people."

The rich in Great Britain, sympathetic to the reactionary outlook of the Confederacy, economically allied with the planters, and jealous of the industrial and commercial competition that the United States already offered and fearful of what she would offer—if still united—in the future, greeted the announcement of emancipation in similar terms.

But among the workers of Great Britain—though now especially suffering because of the Union cotton blockade—the Proclamation was greeted, as Henry Adams, son of the U. S. ambassador, testified, by "a great popular movement." Meetings attended by thousands from mine and mill acclaimed Lincoln and simultaneously denounced their own Tory government and the bosses who dominated it.

In the United States most of the white workers and farming masses, though infected by racism, generally hailed the Proclamation as a blow for human freedom and a means towards hastening peace. Thus, in the border state of Maryland, the *Cambridge Intelligencer,* speaking for non-slaveholders, rejoiced in the Proclamation for it showed the war to be one for freedom. It went on:

> There is another sense in which this is a war of freedom. There are other men in the South to be freed as well as black men . . . The social system of the

South has never been anything short of despotism—a tyranny equal to any of the age. The mind has forever been bound here. Freedom of opinion has never been tolerated below Mason and Dixon's Line . . . Let the mind be free— . . . There can be neither prosperity nor happiness where these are enslaved.

Similarly, a New York City workingmen's paper, *The Iron Platform,* in welcoming Lincoln's Proclamation, pointed out:

There is one truth which should be clearly understood by every working-man in the Union. *The slavery of the black man leads to the slavery of the white man* . . . If the doctrine of treason is true, that "Capital should own Labor," then their logical conclusion is correct, and all laborers, white or black are and ought to be slaves [italics in original].

Of course, the Left—the Abolitionists (including the Marxists)—were pleased with the Proclamation, declaring it to be a document guaranteeing immortality to the man who issued it.

And the Negro people as a whole greeted it, in the words of Frederick Douglass, penned at the time, as "an anthem of the redeemed," "the dawn of a new day," "the answer to the agonizing prayer of centuries."

Dominant American history-writing today, product and bulwark that it is of the status quo, tends, in substance, to agree with the estimates offered by contemporaries hostile to the Proclamation. Naturally, the adverse opinions are expressed without vituperation, but the general verdict conveys the impression that the Proclamation was more sham than reality; that its significance is minor, its issuance demagogic; that its impact, at least at home, was very nearly nil, or, if anything, adverse to the Union.

The reader or student is told that the Proclamation freed no one, that it was "only" a military act, that its actual purpose was simply pro-pagandistic. To this is added the insistence, so general in today's "respectable" historiography, that the war itself was needless, that its outbreak reflected sheer stupidity, that its cause is unknowable, that slavery was benign and truly irrelevant to the war's origin, and that the war's consequences were regrettable. At the same time, the point is conveyed, either by indirection or explicitly, that, in any case, of course, the so-called slaves were Negroes and "everyone" knows what that meant and means in terms of inferiority, docility, and the manifest impossiblity of real liberation since subordination to the superior white represented and represents acceptance of a natural and immutable condition.

A more sentimental version of basically the same chauvinist claptrap—aimed especially at the quite young—is to treat the Proclamation in terms of a gift from on high to the Little Brown Brother through the beneficence of the Great White Father who rather absentmindedly and in the midst of more significant labors deigned to loosen the chains.

Actually, the Emancipation Proclamation is one of the most momentous documents in American history and in the history of the Negro people. As the Declaration of Independence and the Constitution, this document, too, symbolizes and embodies a decisive turning point in our history. It is, indeed, of great consequence in the whole magnificent record of humanity's unceasing effort to throw off oppression and stand forth truly free.

In all this, the centrality of the enslavement of the Negro people is to be observed. Slavery is the fundamental question of pre-Civil War history; it is this fact which made the policy towards slavery of basic consequence during the war itself. Without understanding this it is not possible to understand the Emancipation Proclamation. The widespread *recognition* of the existent fact that the slave question was at the root of the conflict required agitation and guidance and struggle; to get the necessary action to accompany the recognition, to make real the recognition, likewise required constant agitation, alertness, guiding activity and fearless struggle.

The task was complicated by the very great power of the slaveocracy in its homeland and in the North where a thousand economic, political, family, and ideological ties gave it great influence. The task was complicated by the very desperation and fierceness of the slaveholders, attributes characteristic of exploiting classes fighting for their lives. The task was complicated, too, by the neat balance of forces which precariously held the border areas—Delaware, Maryland, Kentucky, much of Tennessee and Virginia (to become West Virginia)—on the side of the Union; these were areas with great manpower, enormous resources and with the only military approaches into the Confederacy.

Complicating too, was the slaveholders' insistence that at stake in an assault upon slavery was the whole concept of the sanctity of contract and the sacredness of private property—"civilization itself," as the phrase went, and still goes. Hence, their insistence that Abolitionism was not only Black Republicanism, but also Red Republicanism, Socialism, agrarianism, levellism, and other epithet-slogans of the moment. Hence their warnings to the well-to-do of the North that if property in slaves goes on Sunday then property in land will go on Monday, and property in factories on Tuesday. If one can be abolished on moral grounds, on the grounds of the welfare of the majority or the improvement of the social order, why not the others on the same grounds, changing only "slave" to "toiling farmer" and to "wage-worker?"

Historically, the reply of the other property owners was: Power is perilous, of course, but it is also delightful. Now you slaveholders hold power and that fact impedes and frustrates our fullest development and keeps *us* out of power. So, we are opposed to your continued domination, a domination based upon the ownership of a type of property extinct among us. Yes, the precedent of attacking property—of any kind, even such as we do not own—is distressing, and we would prefer a gradual dissolution of such property ownership, with generous compensation. But, in any case, power involves risk. You slaveowners have held power and now face its loss; we capitalists will have power—with its risks, no doubt—but we will have it and you will make way for us. We do not mean to destroy you, but we do mean to supersede you. We mean to rule this nation, all of it, with every ounce of its resources, with the entire range of its market, from tip to tip. We will not surrender the Union. We need it all and we will have it all and none will stunt our growth. We want it all for what it offers now, and, magnificent as this is, for the infinite possibilities it will offer in the future.

So, says the new Republican Party, we will not touch slavery where it is. Indeed, we will guarantee its perpetuity, and repeal the Personal Liberty Laws in the North and in other ways see to it that the Fugitive Slave Law is rigidly enforced, but we will not allow the further territorial expansion of slavery by one inch. (On February 27, 1861, the House of Representatives passed a Resolution, 137–53, calling for the repeal of the Personal Liberty Laws and strict enforcement of the Fugitive Slave Act. On February 28, 1861, the House, by 133–65, and the Senate two days later, by 24–12, approved a projected XIII Amendment to the Constitution (the so-called Corwin Amendment) making slavery perpetual *where it was*. Of course, the firing on Fort Sumter made all this merely of historical interest.)

The slaveholding class will not accept this, as later it will not acquiesce in compensated gradual emancipation. The now obsolete ruling class will not peacefully and willingly give up its domination. It will not abide by its own laws, and it finds the democratic implementation of those laws stifling.

Moreover, it knows that no further expansion means not only loss of domination; it means more or less rapid suffocation—it means, in fact, extermination. And this class is keenly aware of how shaky is its power at home; how detested it is by four million slaves, and how despised by seven million non-slaveholding whites. Should it retreat nationally, show weakness, give up domination of the Federal apparatus, could it then hold its own at home—in Alabama, in Georgia?

Even to pose the question was insufferable. No, it would not simply accept defeat; it would not step down. It would fight for "independence," that is, for the perpetuity of a freely expanding slave system, the building of a mighty slave-based empire, the splitting, if not the complete destruction, of the Republic. It would turn to force and violence, to counterrevolution, to real treason.

Finally, it had two more trump cards. One was the great dependence of Western Europe, especially of Great Britain, upon its crops—above all, cotton—and the enormous investments and lucrative connections held by wealthy Britishers in the South. The other was the slavocratic ideology, especially white supremacy, that had pervaded the American atmosphere and permeated the brains of American white people for two centuries. This, played upon by the very real allies of the Confederacy in the North, might so immobilize and weaken Union resistance as to assure the Republic's death.

The young Republican Party was a bourgeois-democratic one and represented a coalition of the industrial bourgeoisie, who exercised hegemony, some merchants, the free farming population, most of the budding working class, the Negro people (there were, in 1860, about 250,000 in the North), almost all the Abolitionists (among whom were the Marxists)—with these components freely critical of official Party policies and statements.

Its policy, reflective of its composition and of the dominant elements of that composition, was extremely vacillating. Its problems were, of course, exceedingly complex and its difficulties very serious and these together help account for much of its hesitancy. Yet, fundamentally, that hesitancy, epitomized in the excruciatingly slow movements of Lincoln, reflected bourgeois concern—even in this progressive phase— over revolutionary activity, especially as such activity seemed to challenge white supremacy. Lincoln, in his First Annual Message to Congress in December 1861, put the matter quite explicitly:

In considering the policy to be adopted for suppressing the insurrection, I have been anxious and careful that the inevitable conflict for this purpose should not degenerate into a violent and remorseless revolutionary struggle. I have, therefore, in every case, thought it proper to keep the integrity of the Union prominent as the primary object of the contest on our part. . . .

Tactically, too, a demand limited to the defense of the Union seemed wisest, for it appeared broadest. No matter how one felt about slavery, no matter how pathological one's hatred for Negroes—the flag was fired upon, the integrity of the Republic was being tested, the destruction of the country was being sought. Rise to defend the flag in a just cause, to preserve the Union, to safeguard your assaulted country. What could be broader than that?

It was the task of the Abolitionists to demonstrate that their program was not narrowing; they had to show that it was not a question of their having a special interest—no matter how noble—to which they were unreasonably attached regardless of all other considerations. It was the task of the Abolitionists to show that they were at least as patriotic as the next man (for a generation, of course, they had been denounced as seditionists, probably in the pay of Great Britain). They had to show that their insistence upon emancipation arose out of that patriotism as well as out of humanism and devotion to democratic principles and a proper concern with rescuing from slavery millions of men, women and children. The Abolitionists had to show that their special devotion to freedom made them *more* perceptive than others of the general needs of the Republic and made them *particularly effective* patriots.

Only a revolutionary policy could defeat the counterrevolutionaries; only a policy directed towards uprooting the key source of the slaveowner's power—slavery—could destroy that power. Why?

1) Because such a policy put an end to the real danger of active intervention on the side of the Confederacy by Western Europe, since the masses there simply would not tolerate or participate in a pro-slavery war.

2) Because such a policy invigorated Northern arms, and where it led to disaffection among officers and men, cleansed the Army by exposing Copperheads.

3) Because such a policy secured the active and full and fervent participation of Negro masses in the struggle—and before the war ended about 230,000 Negro men fought in Lincoln's Army and Navy and about the same number of men and women labored for those services as cooks, scouts, pilots, waggoners, nurses, etc. Without these

scores of thousands of Negro fighters and workers the Union would not have been preserved and slavery would not have been abolished.

4) Because such a policy helped stimulate resistance to slavery and flight from slavery among the plantation masses. Their conspiracies and uprisings, potential and real, tied up thousands of guards and soldiers; their flight reached the stage—as Dr. Du Bois has pointed out—of a mobile general strike, with something like 500,000 succeeding in getting away.

5) Because such a policy deepened disaffection among the non-slaveholding whites in the South. It made increasingly untenable the Bourbons' demagogy about fighting for independence and increasingly clear the fact that the Bourbons were fighting to keep their property and their power—a power oppressive to most Southern whites. The majority of Southern whites opposed secession; their opposition to the Confederacy grew as the war progressed. The policy of emancipation enhanced that opposition, despite the smokescreen of racism, because it helped expose the real purpose of the Confederate ruling class.

Let it be borne in mind that this Emancipation Proclamation—this Executive Act—represented also a clear reversal of the line of "gradualism" and "moderation" that had come so naturally to the largely racist and predominantly bourgeois Republican Party. The original idea had held that the war should be conducted in such a way as to offer the least offense to the slaveowners, who had launched the attack; the first intention was to affirm the irrevelance of slavery to the struggle and to insist that only the integrity of the Union was desired.

But without destroying the traitors, the treason would succeed. And without an anti-slavery policy, the Union would perish, for the strength of those attacking the Union lay in their possession of slaves. To destroy the traitors meant to save the Republic; and to destroy them it was necessary to wage a principled contest in which the deepest Negro-white alliance was forged and in which the stated goal was Negro liberation.

Lincoln was told a thousand times, you "cannot do it"; it was "unthinkable"; the white people would never "stand for it"—these were the alarms raised by the "practical" ones who—somehow—always manage to ally themselves with reaction, albeit, they often say, with a heavy heart. What, it was asked: Recognize Haiti and have Negro Ministers in Washington? Hang a captured slave-trader? Make soldiers of Negroes? Give Negro soldiers equal pay with whites? Have Negro soldiers fight side-by-side with white soldiers, against other white soldiers? Each, it was solemnly asserted, was absolutely impossible; to attempt each was fanatical and mad, and would result only in disaster.

But, Haiti was recognized and her Ministers did come to Washington and the Capitol did not fall down; the slave-trader was hanged, publicly, in New York City, and the Republic did not collapse; Negroes were enlisted in the Army, and the only complaint that persisted was that there were not enough of them; Negro soldiers did fight with white soldiers against Confederate troops and they fought very well, and without them, said Abraham Lincoln and General Grant, it was difficult to see how the Civil War would have ended with a Union victory. The "practical" ones were, in fact, abettors of traitors; the "impractical" radicals were, in fact, decisive contributors to victory and it was the adoption of their program, finally, that made victory possible.

In the past—not to speak of the present epoch—attempts at policies of "too late" and "too little" did not work. All experience shows that when clear, vigorous policies are adopted without equivocation against racial practices, those practices are overcome; *if the object really is social progress and democratic advance,* the policy of "gradualism" and of "moderation" simply does not work.

All this is what the Emancipation Proclamation meant and means. Its meaning is not to be found in its dry listing of counties and parishes and states exempted from its provisions. All that we have indicated is contained within the context of the Proclamation and was actually achieved by struggle in the field; it was maintained and pushed to reality, after the Proclamation, by intensified struggle.

The Abolitionist movement, and the Negro people as a whole, played an indispensable role in transforming the character of the war. From its beginning, people like Frederick Douglass, J. Sella Martin, William Wells Brown, Harriet Tubman, Lucretia Mott, Thaddeus Stevens, Charles Sumner, Wendell Phillips, saw the need of the hour and labored together—men and women, Negro and white—for the liberation of the slaves and the salvation of the Republic. In addition, the grass-roots agitation of the Negro masses to be allowed to get into the fight against the slaveholders was very telling, especially as Union casualties mounted.

Step by step, very slowly, objective necessity—perceived, interpreted, and brought into living reality by courageous people—led Lincoln to pursue a policy of emancipation. *"It must be done. I am driven to it,"* Lincoln wrote to a Pennsylvania Congressman, and he italicized the words. Again, he said to a Kentucky friend: "I was, in my best judgment, driven to the alternative of either surrendering the Union, or of laying strong hold upon the colored element. I chose the latter."

This in no way, of course, withdraws a tittle of the credit due Lincoln. Naturally, the ending of chattel slavery was not the result of one man's will or act, but rather of a whole historic revolutionary process. Yet its final human instrumentality was Abraham Lincoln, that Lincoln who, with all his doubts and his more than touch of racism and all his responsibilities, with all his hesitations and all his terribly difficult problems, did affirm: "I am naturally anti-slavery. If slavery is not wrong, then nothing is wrong."

It is to be added that though Henry Raymond of the *New York Times,* on learning to his displeasure that Lincoln intended to announce emancipation, urged him to do it in the form of a military order, Lincoln did not do so. While his Proclamation twice cited military necessity—an overwhelming reason, surely, in time of war!—it was not cast in the form of an Order, and it concluded by calling the Proclamation "an act of justice" and invoking upon it "the considerate judgment of mankind and the gracious favor of almighty God"—hardly appropriate language for a "mere" military measure.

Lincoln knew that the contest he led was for the preservation of popular sovereignty, of elementary democratic rights, of that government then more highly responsive to public will than any other in the world, of the principles of the Declaration of Independence. This contest he led successfully, not stopping at the revolutionary confiscation of three billion dollars' worth of private property. Of Lincoln, Marx wrote, with his typical sagacity, in March 1862:

> [He] never ventures a step forward before the tide of circumstances and the call of general public opinion forbids further delay. But once "Old Abe" has convinced himself that such a turning point has been reached, he then surprises friend and foe alike by a sudden operation executed as noiselessly as possible.

The Emancipation Proclamation heralded the change of Union strategy from one of futile legalistic defense of the Republic to one of aggressive reestablishment of the integrity of the country by transforming the economy of the enemy and so assuring his military defeat. The Emancipation Proclamation vindicated the policy and program of the

Left; it proved that the policy of "moderation" was a policy of postponement and therefore in fact a policy of acquiescence in the status quo. The Emancipation Proclamation demonstrated, once again and very dramatically, the centrality of the Negro question in all American history. It showed the interdependence of the needs of the Negro people with the needs of general democratic advance. It demonstrated in origin and implementation, the unversality of progressive struggle. International solidarity, personally led by Marx and Engels, was shown to be vital to our own national interest.

The Emancipation Proclamation symbolizes the essence of what Lenin referred to as the "world-historic progressive and revolutionary significance of the American Civil War."

Would that, with the XIII Amendment, the full promise implicit in the Proclamation had really come to pass. Would that the advice offered by the General Council of the First International in an Address to the People of the United States, drafted by Karl Marx, in September 1865, had been followed:

> Injustice against a fraction of your people having been followed by such dire consequences, put an end to it . . .
> The eyes of Europe and the whole world are on your attempts at reconstruction and foes are ever ready to sound the death-knell of republican institutions as soon as they see their opportunity.
> We therefore admonish you, as brothers in a common cause, to sunder all the chains of freedom, and your victory will be complete.

It remains for our generation "to sunder all the chains of freedom." It is our generation, the American working class, the Negro people, the farming masses, the youth, and all democratic-minded people, who will bring to fruition, in the full meaning of our own day—at long last, and after one hundred years—the Emancipation Proclamation.

In this way we shall be continuing into our time the patriotic efforts of those who, a century ago, abolished chattel slavery and preserved our country. We shall be fulfilling Lincoln's promise, uttered at Gettysburg, that this nation "shall have a new birth of freedom."

Published in *Political Affairs*, XXXIV, February 1955, pp. 56–65. Reprinted on "The Centennial of the Emancipation Proclamation," *Political Affairs*, XLII, January 1963, pp. 17–26.

part **II**

HISTORICAL
PERSPECTIVES

4
RACISM AND
CLASS CONSCIOUSNESS

Class Consciousness in the United States

The President of the United States recently remarked that concepts of class struggle were altogether un-American. His motives for saying this are obvious, but that he should have felt it necessary to say this just now reflects the developing militancy of the American working class and the inexorable quality of class struggle, even when covered with the loincloth of "People's Capitalism."

It is not likely, however, that the head of any other capitalist state would have made such a statement. The President's statement reflects a certain national character of rather primitive political development demonstrated most dramatically in the fact that the United States does not have a broadly-based socialist movement; that, indeed, it does not have any national labor party and that its politics are still channelled overwhelmingly within the ruling class confines of the traditional two-party system.

There appears, at least on the surface, to be no real interest in socialism within the organized trade union movement. Indeed, if official statements of union leaders are taken at face value—of course, taking them at face value is wrong—there appears to be a real hostility to socialism in the trade union movement. This is in sharp contrast to the position in other major capitalist countries; and to what existed in the American trade union movement some fifty, even forty years ago.

How shall one explain these peculiarities and apparent paradoxes? What is the reality concerning these matters in the United States today?

The fundamental explanation for the relatively low level of political development and class consciousness among the producing masses in the United States is, substantially, the same as the explanation of a similar phenomenon noted by Engels in Britain some seventy years ago and classically analyzed by Lenin. I refer to the rooting of opportunism and class-collaborationism in imperialism, with the corruption of segments of the metropolitan power's working class, possible for the ruling class on the basis of the super-exploitation of colonial and semi-colonial peoples. This system engenders chauvinism and jingoism, which tend further to divide and weaken the working class.

Yet, while all this is of fundamental importance and must be borne in mind at all times, it remains necessary to inquire further into specifics and peculiarities. So far as the United States is concerned, we should like to draw attention, quite briefly, to certain of the most important of such specifics and peculiarities.

A part of the "New Conservatism"—the ideological mask for cold war reaction—has been a rendering of American history in such a manner as to strip it of its revolutionary content. Notable in this connection has been the influential school of historians who seek to remove even from the American Revolution its revolutionary nature.

Two elements in the Revolution, however, are of especial importance for a proper understanding of the sources of the relatively low level of class consciousness in the United States.

There was, first of all, no real nobility within the rebelling colonies as the result of a nearly total absence of feudalism (there were some exceptions, as in Maryland and upper New York). This tended to reduce the civil-war quality of the Revolution and to lessen the intensity of the internal class struggle. This does not mean that elements of civil war played no part; on the contrary, they were an important part of the Revolution. And class struggle played a no less important part in the origins, conduct and consequences of the Revolution. But both were relatively less notable than was true, for example, of the English Revolution of the seventeenth century, or the French Revolution of the eighteenth century.

There was, secondly, with the success of the Revolution, the widespread acceptance of the idea that now popular sovereignty had come into its own; that, once and for all time, people's revolution had succeeded and henceforward there had only to be vigilance to protect it against reaction. The idea that it might be necessary yet again to have fundamental transformation—to further revolutionize society—seemed anachronistic, or "alien," if not criminal subterfuge for reactionary plotting.

The basic ideas that went into the drafting of the Constitution and the plebiscite which resulted in its adoption seemed to certify that this government was something really altogether new (as in truth it then was) and that finally "government of the people, by the people and for the people" had been established. For large masses of Americans, for many generations, the government was "our government"; many still hold that view.

For about one century the United States was the beacon light of oppressed mankind—"Liberty has fled Europe to find a refuge here," said Thomas Paine; "Send me your huddled masses," said Emma Lazarus in words engraved (with what irony today!) upon our Statue of Liberty. And it was believed that to desire revolution in America was to indicate that one was a newly-arrived immigrant not yet able to shed his "Europeanism."

In everything that has been said above, the reader will notice that the Negro people and the American Indians are omitted. They had no part in this process. In the United States, where there was very little feudalism, there was very much present the pre-feudal social form of chattel slavery until less than 100 years ago. The impact of this upon American life has been enormous, and such is the corrupting power of the poison of white chauvinism that the system of oppression of millions of "free" Negroes exists to this day.

Another consideration connected with the country's origins has had a lasting impact on the quality of its thought and politics. The discovery of America was, of course, a manifestation of the whole historic epoch of the transition from feudalism to capitalism. This New World was viewed as the very embodiment of a fresh start for mankind. It is no accident that the locale of the early Utopias was always set in America. Connected with this was the idea of America as the place where the tenets of the Age of Reason had triumphed.

America seemed to be the fruition of this idea; here a people in the New World had thrown off their shackles, unchained their minds, were free of Lords and Priests, and, led by a remarkable body of statesmen—Jefferson, Madison, the Adamses, Washington, etc.—were establishing a republic that reflected the triumph of Reason in politics.

To all this is added the fact that the United States embodied the typical capitalist notion of freedom as the absence of restraint, rather than the path to social progress. It was widely believed (and still is) that the question of freedom has relevance only to matters of politics and never to matters of economics—since it was insisted that capitalism is freedom in economics.

This and other peculiarities of American origins and patterns of early development have tended to retard the growth of class consciousness.

Much the same applies to certain features of the original American government. Partially for legitimate reasons of defending the Revolution against monarchical and Tory reaction, but fundamentally for reasons of curbing the "excesses" of democracy—that is, the direct participation in government of the masses—the Constitution established a careful "separation of powers," which tends, rather efficiently, to prevent effective manifestation of the popular will. To this was added the "balance wheel" concept of government, so that no group could become predominant and so threaten the republican structure.

The federal structure of government, by increasing the number of sovereignties, has also tended to make more difficult the effective concentration or even development of a popular will, or a popular political organization of nationwide scope. This structure was conceived by Madison as an answer to Aristotle's insistence that democratic government could function only in very limited areas. But Madison's formula was somewhat paradoxical; unity through diversity, a federation of sovereign units. In terms of the needs of a bourgeois democratic republic the arrangement was altogether ingenious; in terms of the active and real participation in politics of the masses of people on a national basis, the arrangement favors the few against the many.

Politically and economically, too, the vast United States has been without a single center; in the United States there is no city comparable to the meaning of Paris to France, or London to England. This, reflecting the great influence of differing regions and sections, has also helped produce a scattering of political effort, and extreme difficulty in the organization of mass national movements and organizations.

The great demographic mobility of the United States also has worked in the same direction. An essential feature of American history has been the process of conquering a continent—and a bloody and ruthless one it has been. In 1790 the geographic center of population in the United

States was east of Baltimore. Today it is in Western Indiana; it has moved about 700 miles west-northwest. The process has been a continous one—over 30 percent of the people do not live in the states of their birth. This is quite apart from the millions and millions who migrated to the United States from Europe, Asia, Africa, Canada and Latin America. This has intensified the diffuseness and relative rootlessness of American life.

The migration of millions from abroad was an important factor in the development of American capitalism. But the resultant divergences in national backgrounds, languages and religions made difficult mass organization. Moreover, because of literacy, residence and other requirements for voting, this mass migration, especially from about 1870 to about 1920, meant that a large proportion of the working class, particularly workers in the basic industries, were in fact without the vote. To this should be added that from 1880 to the present, the majority of the Negro population has also been factually disfranchised, and that since 1895 the majority of poorer Southern whites similarly have been without the vote.

In other words, the American bourgeoisie has had a considerable advantage: the most exploited section of the working masses was in fact deprived of the right to vote. The impact of this upon efforts to form large-scale labor and Negro political parties—or even to bring about large-scale Negro-labor political participation—has been very serious.

And while it is largely true, as we have said, that the United States was relatively free of the classical, European form of feudalism, it is also true that the United States had given the world a classical example of industrial feudalism; i.e., whole towns and communities wherein basic industries are located are the property of giant corporations. The workers' homes, the town's police, the town's churches—quite literally everything is the physical possession of the company. To form elementary trade unions, let alone political organizations, under such circumstances presents the gravest difficulties.

The question of the special oppression of the Negro people is a subject meriting extended discussion. Let it suffice here to say that it, and the chauvinism based upon it, have been important sources for the relative weakness of class consciousness and political organization among the working people of the United States.

A further point must be added: the Southern wing of the Democratic Party has been traditionally, ever since the crushing of the Populist movement in the 1890s, the solid bulwark of reaction. Because of seniority questions and because of the unity of this reactionary bloc, it has acquired exceptional strength. It has been a main source of electoral strength for the Democratic Party, while that Party nationally has tended to be, and is more and more becoming, the Party favored by the labor movement and by the Negroes of the North. This greatly impedes the formation within the United States of a third party of workers, farmers and Negro masses—a party able to smash the bosses' two-party system.

The enormous resources of the United States have been a basic source of the great strength of the bourgeoisie, who have possessed these resources, up to the present. The existence of enormous areas of public lands was important, as Marx noted in the first volume of *Capital,* in making possible, as far back as in colonial days, a relatively higher wage standard than in Europe. The presence of these public lands (up to 1890) played a part in reducing the exacerbation of class struggle. The abundance of other natural resources—coal, iron, oil, gold, silver, copper, lumber, etc.—made possible a lavishness on the part of the American ruling class and a degree of corruption, both in government and in business, that is probably without precedent in human history. This has provided a large amount of crumbs with which to buy off succeeding layers of a labor aristocracy and with which to tempt—too often with success—the intelligentsia.

And this, together with the succeeding waves of immigrants, with each new one tending to fall to the bottom of the social scale (most recently, it has been the Puerto Ricans who have not escaped this fate) has given an appearance of greater "social mobility" than in Europe. And this gave rise to the propaganda stories about America being a land of limitless opportunities—the figure of Horatio Alger is an American one, and the optimistic axiom "from rags to riches" also is American. This, of course, has been basically ruling class mythology; but it has penetrated and has merged into the national psychology.

Incidentally, this should help explain why Social Darwinism has had so large and long a vogue in the United States. William Graham Sumner, for forty years a professor of sociology at Yale University, produced a widely-read book in 1883 called *What Social Classes Owe to Each Other.* In it he insisted that the answer was—nothing. That is, Sumner insisted that the rich were rich because they were better than the poor, and the poor were poor because they were no good. He insisted on the "natural" quality of capitalism and its ruthless laws of self-adjustment which might be tinkered with, by fools, at grave peril to social order and social well-being. Significantly, the book appeared at a time of serious ferment among workers, farmers, Negroes and others of the exploited. Its appearance reaffirmed the existence of class struggle in the United States, which no amount of theorizing has been able to exorcize.

Nevertheless, the professor's book, and the arguments it advanced, have had substantial influence on the American mind. Not only is it true that poverty is held to be shameful—this is a normal judgment in an exploitative society where to have money is to be "successful." It is also true that too often those who are poor actually feel ashamed of that fact. During the great depression of the 1930s, for instance, one of the stumbling blocks in organizing the unemployed was their sense of shame at being without a job, of being "failures."

War-making has been a basic attribute of all exploitative societies. That applies with great force to the American experience.

The conquest of the present continental territory of the United States was accompanied by war—against the Indians, wars were waged from the early seventeenth century until the closing years of the nineteenth century. At the same time the whole institution of slavery had about it much of a warlike nature, and in it the savage repression of the slaves was a permanent feature. From these "internal" wars the American bourgeoisie derived enormous wealth and profit.

Even more profitable were the wars against Mexico, Spain, the Philippines, and both world wars. Except for the Civil War of 1861–65 (and even that touched directly only one-third of the country), the United States has not felt the impact of war on its own soil. From all of these wars and the numerous "interventions" the bourgeoisie has profited enormously; at the same time wars were devastating large areas of Latin America, Europe and Asia and helped American capital penetrate the rest of the world, especially Europe.

The wars also helped arouse nationalism and jingoism and turn the minds of the masses away from domestic problems and issues— especially since, with the partial exception of the Korean adventure, the United States has never been defeated in war. [This essay, of course, was written more than a decade before the defeat of the United States in Vietnam. For Aptheker's assessment of the triumph of the liberation forces in Vietnam see his essay: "Vietnam Cease-Fire: Historic Turning Point," *Political Affairs,* LII (March, 1973): pp. 41–52.—Editor]

In the postwar period, the Korean "police action" and the Cold War have served as a pretext for the ruling class to demand "national unity" in the face of the "emergency." They have served also as the excuse for military expenditures that in their total are quite without precedent. Thus, since 1947 the United States government has spent about 500 billion dollars for direct war expenditures.

All this has been adroitly exploited by the bourgeoisie to mute class consciousness. Capitalist economists insist that without these colossal expenditures it would be impossible to maintain "prosperity." That and similar theories have had a considerable influence in developing opportunism and class collaborationism among leadership elements in the trade union movement. With few exceptions, the top union leaders support the aggressive and expansionistic foreign policy.

The connection between opportunism in the labor movement and imperialism is especially apparent in the United States. We know that the relatively high living standards enjoyed by the top layer of workers are the result of super-exploitation of the colonies.

However, in the United States, to this must be added the enormous tribute brought into the country by its economic domination and exploitation of the "free" world, which is to say, that part of the world which may still be "freely" exploited by American capital. American investments abroad total more than those of all other capitalist countries combined, and in the past ten years they have grown at an unprecedented pace.

Capitalist prosperity, however shaky it may be, however partial are its benefits, remains the greatest single source of class collaborationism. With so-called prosperity, this policy seems to "pay off," as we say in the United States. This is an illusion, but one that strongly induces opportunism.

A witty French friend, visiting the United States, remarked to me, paraphrasing Lincoln Steffens's remark anent the U.S.S.R.: "I have seen the past, and it works." So long as it seems "to work"—particularly given the pragmatic bent of Americans—the people will more or less abide by it.

And the ruling class is doing everything to make them abide by it. It maintains an enormous propaganda campaign against Marxism, socialism, communism and the socialist countries. Without a doubt, this subject is discussed and written about more than any other, with the possible exception of pornographic subjects which form the backbone of American "letters" today.

Together with the propaganda go social and economic pressure. To be a partisan of Marxism is to be a pariah; to be known as a radical is to invite beggary; to be a Communist is to invite persecution. The Communist Party has been driven into semi-legality by the U. S. government; today three members of its National Committee are still in jail; most of the remaining members recently have been in jail and are still under indictment. The Party's 78-year-old Honorary Chairman, William Z. Foster, confined to bed for the past years as a result of severe illness, is still under indictments a dozen years old, and is not allowed to obtain proper care and treatment in the socialist countries.

The trade union movement has been harried with anti-communism of an official and unofficial kind. Individual states have passed laws aimed against progressive ideas. And the FBI maintains a dossier on literally millions of Americans who at some point in their lives supported Republican Spain, or urged the boycott of Imperial Japan, or have Negro friends, or were militant trade unionists, or otherwise conducted themselves in a manner displeasing to Edgar Hoover.

A refurbished Cold War ideology has made its appearance to justify all of the above repression and to prepare for the realization of The American Century. This New Conservatism, which has even secularized the concept of original sin, insists upon the essential and immutable rottenness of mankind. It preaches an elitism that denies basic precepts of democratic theory; it insists that bureaucratism characterize all forms of social organization; it denies basic elements of the Age of Reason, such as the concept of causation and the idea of progress. It breeds cynicism and apathy; it laughs at devotion and social concern as manifestations of idiocy or criminality; it repudiates all value judgments; it spits at life as one vast delusion.

That is one method of mass corruption. Another is racism. All this tends to give to much of American life, especially in the large cities, an air of extreme tension and fierce competitiveness. All these together foster very high rates of crime, especially among the youth, suicide, drug addiction, alcoholism and other forms of "social escape." The spread of mental illness is undoubtedly connected with this. Half the beds in American hospitals are occupied by the mentally ill; it has been statistically estimated that one out of ten Americans now living will at some point in their lives enter an institution for the mentally sick!

Institutions of social welfare and care are in crisis throughout the country. Even Professor John K. Galbraith, in his very one-sided book,

The Affluent Society, emphasizes that in the midst of all this alleged "affluence," institutions and services of a public welfare character are in decay. Thus, slums are increasing at the rate of 4 percent per year, and what housing construction is going on is devoted almost entirely to fulfilling the needs of the rich and the upper middle class. Hospitals are scandalously overcrowded; so are schools—and so are prisons. In the latter, riots and rebellions are a weekly occurrence. No wonder that in the United States, politicians, ministers, and editorial writers are alluding more and more often to the decline and fall of the Roman Empire!

With all the "prosperity" and all the talk about "people's capitalism," since World War II there have been three economic cycles in the United States, and the recession of each succeeding one has been more prolonged and deeper than the others. The last (1957–58) was the most prolonged and the deepest. And with each recovery, the number remaining totally unemployed increases; today the government itself admits 3.3 million altogether out of work. The figure is an underestimate. [In 1976, government figures showed 8.8 million people unemployed.—Editor]

While the "people's capitalism" propaganda alleges the end of monopolization of ownership and control, the fact is that monopolization has been considerably accelerated, as evidenced by the numerous bank mergers. And while the propaganda holds that all Americans are owners of shares in the corporate economy, official data for 1956 showed that only 5 percent of the population owned stock, actually a lower percentage than in the 1930s, when about 7 percent of the population owned shares. Since World War II, in fact, there has been a sharpening of class polarization. The process is described, albeit rather superficially, in the recent best seller, *The Status Seekers,* by Vance Packard.

In the land where "poverty has been eliminated," the Census Bureau reported that in 1956 the median family income per year was $4,237. This was the unadjusted dollar (taking no account of the postwar inflation), before taxes which take up at least 25 percent of the average family income. This source showed that, as of 1956, the income of 34.5 percent of American families was less than $3,000 per year. [Statistics in 1975 provided by various government agencies show that the tendency toward the relative *and absolute* impoverishment of the working class in the United States continues, and at an accelerated rate.—Editor]

Yet, according to the U.S. Department of Labor, in 1956 a family of four needed a minimum annual income of about $4,400. Other estimates, as those of the Heller Committee of the University of California, reported the needed income to be about $5,000 a year. Taking either estimate, over one-third of the population lives in families whose annual income, before taxes, is less than $3,000. How far has the United States come, with all the boasting about unparalleled "prosperity," from Franklin Delano Roosevelt's "one-third of a nation" that was "ill-fed, ill-housed, ill-clothed?"

And, it must be added, the U.S. government figures show the median annual income of Negro families in 1956 came to $2,289. Let it not be forgotten that there are about nineteen million Negroes in the United States.

It is a basic truth that there exist in the United States workers and bosses; those who own the means of production and those who do not. Hence, in the States, too, the Marxist analysis of capitalism fully applies. And that it is vindicated there, too, where the bourgeoisie have been especially favored, demonstrates its universality.

What one has in the United States, therefore, is not the *absence* of class consciousness, but a *relatively lower pace* of development of class consciousness, which most recently has been rising. This consciousness has reached the point, despite the particular circumstances outlined above, of large-scale union organization, of increasing strikes, of rising militancy and of growing indications of political independence on the part of the working class. This latter fact—especially shown in the elections of November 1958—is acutely worrying the ruling class and its favorite politicians.

Objective needs, particularly of the working class and the Negro people, force the appearance of opposition to ruling-class policy. This has been rising in the area of domestic politics; what is new is that it has been gathering momentum in the area of foreign policy. Increasingly, the excuse of "emergency" is wearing thin; the propaganda about the "Soviet menace" is growing stale; and the conviction is spreading that a modern major war would be so catastrophic that it simply must never be permitted. The average American is coming to realize that any foreign policy directed against the U.S.S.R. and People's China, threatening to involve the United States in a war with those powers, is simply insane so far as the real interests of the American people are concerned.

At the same time, popular resistance broke the back of the worst features of McCarthyism, though its vestiges are many and serious. The libertarian and militant traditions of the American people cannot be so easily turned into their opposite, as the ruling class would like. Thus, on the cultural and ideological fronts there has been mounting resistance to reaction and to the New Conservatism so that today, unlike three or four years ago, the latter ideology by no means fully dominates.

Nor has the bourgeoisie been able to smash the organized Marxist-Leninist component in the United States. There was dire crisis in the Communist Party in 1956-57, and some of its consequences are still being felt. But the crisis is over, the worst is overcome. The Party lives and is regaining strength. It has a great, an historic, role to play and its science, devotion and leadership are needed by the working class, the Negro people and the masses generally in the United States.

Published in *New Times* (Moscow) number 44 and 47, 1959. Reprinted as a pamphlet, *Class Consciousness in the United States* (New York: Jefferson Bookshop, 1959).

White Chauvinism: The Struggle Inside the Ranks

White chauvinism is a problem only for the exploited; for the exploiters it is a weapon—carefully forged and regularly refurbished.

The ideology of white supremacy is not new; on the contrary it was born of slavery and has been American reaction's trump card for three centuries. The struggle against it also is not new and progressives today who understand this to be a life and death matter would do well to study something of that history.

As a beginning toward this aim I shall examine some of the evidences of the presence of white supremacist thinking within two of the major progressive efforts of the past—the Abolitionist and the early labor movements—and shall focus attention upon the struggles against this evil conducted by Negro participants.

The entire movement against chattel slavery was permeated with the fight against white supremacist thinking. For essential to that system was its rationalization—"if it could be proved," said a slaveholder to the visiting English author, Harriet Martineau, "that Negroes are more than a link between man and brute, the rest follows of course, and I must liberate all of mine."

From before the Revolution to the enactment of the Thirteenth Amendment Negroes devoted themselves to refuting this slander. You complain of British tyranny, wrote "An African" to the American colonists in 1774, but "Are not your hearts also hard, when you hold men in slavery who are entitled to liberty by the law of nature, equal as yourselves? . . . pray, pull the beam out of thine own eye, that you may see clearly to pull the mote out of my brother's eye." "There could be nothing more natural," wrote the Negro Abolitionist, Hosea Easton, in 1837, "than for a slave-holding nation to indulge in a train of thoughts and conclusions that favored their idol, slavery. . . . 'The love of money is the root of all evil'; it will induce its votaries to teach lessons to their little babes, which only fits them for the destroyers of their species in this world, and for the torments of hell in the world to come." And , in 1860, a committee of New York Negroes, in appealing for universal male suffrage, asked questions terribly relevant today: "What stone has been left unturned to degrade us? What hand has refused to fan the flame of popular prejudice against us? What American artist has not caricatured us? What wit has not laughed at us in our wretchedness? What songster has not made merry over our depressed spirits? What press has not ridiculed and condemned us? Few, few, very few. . . ."

Such an atmosphere was not without its effect upon white Abolitionists: many of them thought of the Negro as not quite human, or as childish, stupid, meek. There developed within the movement an attitude of toleration, an air of patronage, a feeling of condescension, and among the many invaluable contributions of the Negro Abolitionists to that movement was their persistent struggle against this racism.

The very first editorial of the earliest Negro newspaper *(Freedom's Journal,* New York, March 16, 1827) rather gently, but still firmly, remarked that "our friends . . . seem to have fallen into the current of popular feeling and are imperceptibly floating on the stream—actually living in the practice of prejudice, while they abjure it in theory. . . . Is it not very desirable that such should know more of our actual condition;

and of our efforts and feelings, that in forming or advocating plans for our amelioration, they may do it more understandingly?"

Characteristic were the impassioned remarks of Reverend Theodore S. Wright before the 1837 convention of the New York Anti-Slavery Society. There, insisting upon the falseness of white superiority and the presence of its advocates within the Abolitionist movement, Wright said: "I fear not all the machinations, calumny and opposition of slaveholders, when contrasted with the annexation of men" with such views. "These points," he continued, "which have lain in the dark must be brought out to view. . . . It is an easy thing to ask about the vileness of slavery at the South, but to call the dark man a brother . . . to treat the man of color in all circumstances as a man and brother—that is the test." He went on at length: "I am sensible I am detaining you, but I feel that this is an important point" for he knew that "men can testify against slavery at the South, and not assail it at the North, where it is tangible. . . . What can the friends of emancipation effect while the spirit of slavery is so fearfully prevalent? Let every man take his stand, burn out this prejudice, live it down . . . and the death-blow to slavery will be struck."

One of the most persistent manifestations of white superiority within the Abolitionist movement was the assumption that its white members were to do its "thinking," with the Negroes appearing as exhibits or puppets. Among certain of the whites there was a feeling that they were to do the writing and editing, formulate policy, devise strategy; the Negroes were to assist where they could, improve—and keep on fleeing the patriarchal paradise! Negro Abolitionists did not fail to denounce this arrogance and to insist upon the terrible injury it was doing to the cause.

A prime example of this occurred in 1843 in connection with a Negro National Convention held in Buffalo. Here a leading Abolitionist, Henry Highland Garnet, proposed that the convention urge the slaves to go on a general strike demanding freedom, and that, when the demand was rejected and the masters attempted to break the strike with violence, the slaves answer this with insurrection. After prolonged debate, the convention rejected—by one vote—the proposal.

Most of the white Abolitionists were then still largely tied to the Garrisonian ideas of moral suasion as the only proper anti-slavery method and so denounced Garnet's idea. This, Garnet received as an honest difference of opinion, but when certain of the whites expressed *scorn* for the thinking of the convention that was something else again. And when Mrs. Maria Weston Chapman, a well-known poet of the period and, in Garrison's absence, acting editor of *The Liberator,* organ of the American Anti-Slavery Society, took a similar position and added her fears that Mr. Garnet had "received bad counsel," she was favored with a scorching reply. Garnet, himself an escaped slave, reminded Mrs. Chapman that no one knew slavery so well as a slave and that those who had escaped came "to tell you, and others, what the monster has done and is still doing." Moreover, he went on, "You say that I 'have received bad counsel.' You are not the only person who has told your humble servant that his humble productions have been produced by the 'counsel' of some Anglo-Saxon. I have expected no more from ignorant slaveholders and their apologists, but I really looked for better things from Mrs. Maria W. Chapman. . . ." For Mrs. Chapman it is to be said that Garnet's letter was published promptly in *The Liberator* and unquestionably had a salutary effect.

The patronizing attitude was also an important factor in the opposition which cropped up within the Abolitionist movement to the frequent and vital city, state, regional and national Negro conventions and societies that played a key role in the struggle against slavery and discrimination. This, too, was part of the hostility within anti-slavery groups to the establishment of newspapers and magazines by Negroes themselves. It is to a great degree what Frederick Douglass had in mind when, in the first number of his Rochester newspaper, *The North Star* (December 3, 1847)—the establishment of which met much hostility from the Garrisonians—he declared that he had begun the paper not from a feeling of "distrust or ungrateful want of appreciation of the zeal, integrity or ability of the noble band of white laborers in this department or our cause." Rather, he had done this because of the fact "that the man who has *suffered the wrong* is the man to *demand redress*—that the man *struck* is the man to *cry out*—and that he who has *endured the cruel pangs of slavery* is the man to *advocate liberty*. It is evident," he concluded, that "we must be our own representatives and advocates, not exclusively, but peculiarly; not distinct from, but in connection with our white friends. In the grand struggle for liberty and equality now waging, it is meet, right and essential that there should arise in our ranks authors and editors, as well as orators, for it is in these capacities that the most permanent good can be rendered to our cause."

It is this same weakness, this failure to insist upon the absolute equality of the Negro, which is important in understanding the decision of the majority of those in the American Anti-Slavery Society to disband in May 1865, when the demise of chattel slavery was clear. The Negro delegates to the Society's convention of that year—like Robert Purvis and Frederick Douglass—opposed the move. They pointed out that the constitution of the organization called for the elimination of discrimination as well as slavery and they insisted that freedom for the Negro was still very far from complete both in the North and in the South. Until, said Douglass, the Negro in the South had full political, economic and social equality and until jim crow vestiges of slavery had been abolished throughout the land, the national society dedicated to these aims should hold together and fight. Slavery, he said, "has been called by a great many names, and it will call itself by yet another name; and you and I and all of us had better wait and see what new form this old monster will assume, in what new skin this old snake will come forth."

When it is realized that such an appeal did not convince a majority of even so advanced a group as the American Anti-Slavery Society, it should be clear how significant to the aborting of Reconstruction was the failure among progressive groups, to grasp the key importance of the Negro question.

The same failing has plagued the labor movement since its inception. After the Civil War, with its destruction of chattel slavery, its preservation of bourgeois democracy and the integrity of the nation and its tremendous boost to industrialization, the trade union movement leaped forward. But from the beginning white supremacist thinking and behavior crippled it. And from the beginning it was the Negro who most clearly saw and most persistently pointed out the necessity of unity and who, in the cause of this unity, attacked all signs of chauvinism.

A very early post-Civil War strike in the South illustrates the condition. In 1866 the white bricklayers of New Orleans, having formed a jim crow union, struck for higher wages. Negroes continued working and the bosses filled the places of the strikers by hiring more. As a result the strikers issued a call for a general meeting of all bricklayers and the Negro newspaper, the New Orleans *Tribune,* organ of the Radical Republican party, editorialized: "We hope that the colored bricklayers, before entering into any movement with their white companions, will demand, as a preliminary measure, to be admitted into the benevolent and other societies which are in existence among white bricklayers. As peers, they may all come to an understanding and act in common. But should the white bricklayers intend to use their colored comrades as tools, and simply to remove the stumbling block they now find in their way, without guaranty for the future, we would say to our colored brethren: keep aloof, go back to your work, and insist upon being recognized as men and equals before you do anything."

This particular effort and strike failed and it failed precisely because the white workers, poisoned as they were, failed to recognize "their colored comrades . . . as men and equals."

The pattern repeated itself in the history of the first national federation of trade unions in this country, the National Labor Union, founded in 1866 under the leadership of William H. Sylvis. Indeed, Sylvis' own greatest weakness, which so tragically vitiated his fine qualities—class consciousness, enormous energy, personal honesty and great administrative ability—was white chauvinism. (In his "Letters from the South," published in the Philadelphia *Workingmen's Advocate* (1869), Sylvis consistently calumniated the Negro—while formally calling, within the N.L.U., for Negro-white unity!)

What was true of Sylvis was true of the National Labor Union. In 1866, 1867 and 1868 it refused to accept Negroes though the issue was brought to the fore by the independent organizing activities of Negro workers, their calls for unity and the awareness of the need for such unity from certain of the white leaders. Finally, with the accumulations of all these pressures, which brought Sylvis himself to call more actively for Negro-white unity, nine Negroes were seated among the total of 142 delegates to the 1869 convention of the National Labor Union. These Negroes, representing hod carriers, caulkers, molders, railroad workers and painters were led by the greatest pioneer figure in the history of Negro trade union organization, Isaac Myers, a Baltimore caulker.

In Philadelphia on August 18, 1869, Isaac Myers, speaking, as he said, for all the Negro delegates, made one of the most significant addresses in American history, and while he spoke, reported the *New York Times,* he was "listened to with the most profound attention and in perfect silence."

"Gentlemen," he began, "silent but powerful and far-reaching is the revolution inaugurated by your act in taking the colored laborer by the hand and telling him that his interest is common with yours, and that he should have an equal chance in the race for life." Unity, unity on the basis of equality, was the essence of his message; that and nothing else would guarantee the potency of the American trade union movement. "I speak today," he concluded, "for the colored men of the whole country, from the lakes to the Gulf, from the Atlantic to the Pacific— from every hill-top, valley and plain throughout our vast domain— when I tell you that all Negroes ask for themselves is a fair chance; that you shall be no worse off by giving them that chance; that you and they will dwell in peace and harmony together; that you and they may make one steady and strong pull until the laboring men of this country shall receive such pay for time made as will secure them a comfortable living for their families, educate their children and leave a dollar for a rainy day and old age. Slavery, or slave labor, the main cause of the degradation of white labor, is no more. And it is the proud boast of my life that the slave himself had a large share in the work of striking off the fetters that bound him by the ankle, while the other end bound you by the neck."

Though this stimulated the adoption of good resolutions by the convention and the appointment of a Negro organizer, the resolutions were not implemented and the organizer was not used. Negroes shortly thereafter, again led by Myers, held their own convention of the Colored National Labor Union, in Washington from December 6–10, 1869. Over 200 delegates attended from Negro organizations and trade unions in twenty-three states including eleven in the South. In their address to the American people they insisted they opposed "discrimination as to nationality, sex, or color." "Any labor movement," they asserted, "based upon such discrimination . . . will prove to be of very little value." Indeed, it would be "suicidal" for it would encourage "dissensions and divisions which in the past have given wealth the advantage over labor." Specifically urged was a common phalanx of the Irish and German and Chinese, the Northern mechanic and the Southern poor white, men and women—all who labor and had been "so long ill taught" that their "true interest is gained by hatred and abuse of the laborer of African descent."

How pertinent for the American labor movement today is this call from the doubly-exploited, and therefore doubly-sensitive, Negro workers of eighty years ago!

The immediate post-Civil War labor movement failed and among the several reasons for this is the influence of white supremacist thinking within the workers' organizations.

A somewhat similar course marks the record of the next great national labor organization in American history—the Knights of Labor. Here, however, the degree of Negro-white unity achieved was considerably greater than within the National Labor Union. The Knights, founded secretly in 1869 because of boss hostility and persecution, grew through the early seventies, maintained a precarious existence through the terrible years of the "Long Depression" (1873–79) and expanded mightily in the next decade. Class conscious in its vigorous years, militant, organized along industrial lines and welcoming women and Negro workers, it had by the middle eighties something like 650,000 members.

However, this organization by no means made a complete break with white supremacist thinking or conduct and maintained jim crow, as well as some mixed locals, but it did have about 70,000 Negroes. That at least 10 percent of the Knights were Negroes—when Negroes totalled about 13 percent of the population, with the vast majority in agriculture, domestic service or other occupations largely untouched by unionization—speaks well for the degree of unity achieved and the eagerness of Negro workers to enter unions.

Evidences of the overcoming of white chauvinism, especially when this took the form of concrete action, were hailed by the Negro people. Thus, in October 1886, a New York Negro wrote: "I had a letter sent me from Georgia by a colored man asking if colored men would be recognized in the Knights of Labor, and I have had similar questions from others of my race. . . . My answer is Yes. . . . I myself belong to a local that is wholly composed of white men, with two exceptions, and I hold a very high position of trust in it. . . . I will say to my people, Help the cause of labor. I would furthermore say to colored men, Organize. . . . Let us break this race prejudice which capital likes. Let us put our shoulders to the wheel as men and victory is ours."

Ida B. Wells, a courageous Negro newspaper woman of Memphis, wrote early in 1887 of having attended a local meeting of the Knights. "I noticed," she commented, "that everyone who came was welcomed and every woman from black to white was seated with the courtesy usually extended to white ladies alone in this town. It was the first assembly of the sort in this town where color was not the criterion to recognition as ladies and gentlemen. Seeing this," she added, "I could listen to their enunciation of the principles of truth and justice and accept them with a better grace than all the sounding brass and tinkling cymbal of a minister, even though expounded in a consecrated house and over the word of God."

Nevertheless, jim crow locals existed and much of the top leadership, including the Grand Master Workman, Terence V. Powderly, were quite opportunist on this question. Increasingly as compromising tactics developed in the Knights in face of burgeoning monopoly capitalism, the deterioration faithfully reflected itself on the Negro question.

Typical of the keen awareness of this disastrous change was the letter, written in the summer of 1887, by a Pittsburgh Negro steel worker. So significant and characteristic is this document that I will quote it at some length. "As a strike is now in progress at the Black Diamond Steel Works, where many of our race are employed," wrote the worker, "the colored people hereabouts feel a deep interest in its final outcome. As yet few colored men have taken any part in it, it having been thus far thought unwise to do so. It is true our white brothers, who joined the Knights of Labor and organized the strike without conferring with, or in any way consulting us, now invite us to join with them and help them to obtain the desired increase in wages. . . . But as we were not taken into their scheme at its inception and as it was thought by them that no trouble would be experienced in obtaining what they wanted without our assistance, we question very much the sincerity and honesty of this invitation. . . . I am not opposed to organized labor. God forbid that I should be when its members are honest, just, and true! But when I join any society, I want to have pretty strong assurance that I will be treated fairly. . . . If white workers will take the colored man by the hand and convince him by actual fact that they will be true to him and not a traitor to their pledge, he will be found with them ever and always; for there are not under heaven men in whose breasts beat truer hearts than in the breast of the Negro."

The status of American labor in our own time demonstrates the exact truth of the words of this Negro steel worker written in 1887—*"If white workers will take the colored man by the hand and convince him by actual fact that they will be true to him and not a traitor to their pledge, he will be found with them ever and always."*

In concluding this brief survey of the efforts of Negroes to combat white chauvinism within two of the greatest people's movements in our history I reemphasize that this barely touches the general subject. A history of white chauvinism would delve fully into its basic socio-economic origins, and trace the appearance and development of its numerous stereotypes and manifestations. It would examine its impact upon the totality of American life, and would shed new light on every major facet of our past. From such a study fuller understanding would emerge of the Revolution, the Civil War, Reconstruction, the numerous third party movements (and especially the Populist movement), the fight for women's rights, the battle against imperialism, the development of socialism.

White chauvinism today is the specific tool of American imperialism. That imperialism is the main bulwark of world reaction; therefore the struggle against this chauvinism, led by the Communist Party, assumes world-wide significance. During the Civil War the life of the nation depended upon Negro-white unity; today that remains true, and, in addition, the universal fight against fascism and war requires this Negro-white unity. The duty and necessity for this struggle, devolving first of all upon the American white masses is, then, crystal-clear. On the success with which Negro-white unity is forged depends, quite literally, the firm establishment of world peace and the progress of our country towards democracy and socialism.

Published in *Masses & Mainstream,* III, February 1950, pp. 47–57.

The History of Anti-Racism in the United States: An Introduction

There is, of course, an abundant literature on the nature, history and defenses of slavery in the United States and on the history of the movements against slavery. There exists, also, a considerable literature on racism in the United States; its origins, nature, institutional forms, purpose and function. There is in addition some extant writings—not very much—on efforts to eliminate reflections of racism, as struggles against peonage, against jim crow, and against specific forms of racist practices, as in travel, education, employment, and housing.

There is, however, almost no literature treating of the history of *anti-racist thought* in the United States; indeed, so far as I know, there is no single book devoted to this subject and precious few articles that deal with it in any way.

Certainly, works treating of anti-slavery—as example, that by Dwight Lowell Dumond in his later writings, of W. E. B. Du Bois, Charles H. Wesley, Louis Ruchames, Thomas E. Drake, John Hope Franklin, Benjamin Quarles, James M. McPherson and me—have brought forward evidences of anti-racist views but this was neither sustained nor systematic; where it appears, it tended or tends to be incidental rather than fundamental in even these writings.

Similarly, in studies of racism one will certainly find references to rejection of this ideology, but the works are studies of racism, not its opposition, as the very title, for example, of Winthrop Jordan's book makes clear: *White Over Black: American Attitudes Toward the Negro, 1550-1812* (1968).

The point here is that "white over black" was *one* of the attitudes of (white) Americans toward the Negro; one not only had the Black person's attitude toward himself—which, of course, is very much a part of "the American attitude"—but one also had attitudes toward Black people by non-Black people living in the United States which was not one of superiority but rather was one of either questioning the stance of superiority or of rejecting it, and in some cases rejecting it passionately.

There are a few partial exceptions to this rule. For example, James M. McPherson's *The Struggle for Equality: Abolitionists and the Negro in the Civil War and Reconstruction* (1964), especially on pages 134-53, treats of opposition to racism; less effectively, Thomas F. Gossett in his *Race: The History of an Idea in America* (1963), in his final two chapters, also deals with opposition, but neither book is meant to be a history of anti-racism. The book which comes closest to presenting racist and anti-racist argumentation is Louis Ruchames' excellent reader, *Racial Thought in America,* of which only the first volume has been published as of this writing: *From the Puritans to Abraham Lincoln* (1969).

One might wonder whether the absence of a body of literature on anti-racism in the United States is not due to an absence of anti-racism in the country? The evidence is against this view. It shows, on the contrary, that just as slavery induced both its defense and its attack, so racism induced both its defense and its refutation, but the literature presents the former and largely has ignored the latter. It is past time this neglect was overcome.

Ulrich Bonnell Phillips, the late chief apologist for the slave system in the United States, insisted that white supremacy and the effort to maintain it was basic to Southern history; in our own day, Eugene D. Genovese has agreed with him. Prof. James M. McPherson not only agrees with Phillips on this point, but adds racism as a fundamental current generally in U. S. history; that was the view, also, of the late Allan Nevins.

In both cases, I believe the view is wrong. Both make the South, white, and make the nation, white—in any active sense; both make the white South monolithic and the white nation monolithic and in both cases this is altogether wrong; and the Phillipsian-Nevins-Genovese-McPherson view gives to Southern history and to national history a static quality; that is, a quality whose essence is the maintenance of the status quo, instead of one whose essence was and is a *struggle* to maintain that status quo *and a struggle to change it.* It is this fully dynamic quality which has characterized both Southern and national history. (I published a critique of the Phillipsian view as to "the central theme of Southern history" in 1956, in my *Toward Negro Freedom,* pp. 182-91.)

In a provocative essay, "The Proslavery Argument Revisited," Ralph E. Morrow suggested *(Mississippi Valley Historical Review,* June 1961), that its purpose was not so much to persuade Northern white people of the justice of slavery, but rather to persuade *Southern* white people—and especially the youth and intelligentsia of the ruling circles among such people—of the justice of slavery.

Quite recently, Anne F. Scott has argued persuasively that this propaganda did not convince the *women* among the slaveowning class of the South; that they seem to have been anti-slavery—or, at least, that many of them were. That is the point of her essay, "Women's Perspective on the Patriarchy in the 1850's," in *The Journal of American History* (June 1974). Present is the implication, at least, that this difference in viewpoint concerning the enslavement of Black people had its origin in the realities of their own subordinate position in the "patriarchy" known as Dixie.

This ruling-class sense of urgency in terms of persuading their own white population—young and old, men and women, rich and poor—of the justness of a pro-slavery and racist ideology was intensified because that ruling class dominated a blatantly male chauvinist, elitist and oligarchic social order, all of which produced moods of acute doubt and actions of protest and even, at times, near-rebellion. Add to this the originally fraternal and revolutionary character of Christianity and the intensely egalitarian and democratic essence of the verbiage in the Declaration of Independence and one can understand, I suggest, something of the almost frantic tone to the slavocratic and racist propaganda that issued forth incessantly from figures like Dew, Fitzhugh, De Bow, Calhoun, et al.

Might one not suggest that if much of the urgency of the argument for slavery derived out of the strength of anti-slavery ideas—in the South as well as elsewhere—then perhaps the extraordinary intensity of racist argumentation may derive in part at least, out of the existence of anti-racist ideas?

To be opposed to slavery—even less, to be opposed to the rule of the slaveowners—did not mean, of course, that one was opposed to racism. To reject racism was a profoundly deep rejection of the entire extant social order; this is true in the United States at the end of the twentieth century and it was markedly true in the preceding three centuries. This makes all the more significant the fact that there was in those centuries rather widespread questioning of racism and even considerable rejection of it.

The history of anti-slavery begins with the first slave; similarly, the history of anti-racism begins with the original object of scorn, derision and insult. In addition, just as the anti-slavery movement was not confined to slaves or to Black people, so anti-racism was not confined to the immediate objects of its attack. Du Bois once remarked that the history of the United States in large part consisted of the position and treatment of Black people and the response thereto; in similar vein one may affirm that racism and the struggle against it constitute a significant component of and, in many ways, a basic axis around which revolves much of the history of the United States. This is especially true if one understands racism as organically tied to the socio-economic base of society and the struggle against it as constituting therefore a fundamental aspect of the effort to transform—to revolutionize—that society.

A history of anti-racism, in any complete sense, would reflect opposition to racist attitudes and practices towards the Indian and the African and the Afro-American. In addition, one has in the United States racist views expressed against—and these views combatted—Mexican and Mexican-derived peoples, Puerto Rican people and more generally Latin-American peoples; against Asian peoples, with some shades of differences as applied to Filipino, Chinese and Japanese peoples, for example; against Jewish people, especially after about 1870 and particularly Jewish people from Eastern Europe; against Irish people; and peoples from Eastern and Southern Europe, especially Italian and Slavic peoples.

While all this would not be the entirety of U. S. history, of course, it would make up a large part of it and it does constitute a basic component of that history—*but it has not been written.* This racism and anti-racism have significantly affected *all* areas of U. S. history, foreign and domestic, from religion to education, from war-making to treaty-making, from the arts to politics, from trade union activity to women's struggles, from medicine to anthropology to psychology, from taxation policy to police practices, from jurisprudence to dramaturgy.

In this particular essay, I am suggesting the crucial significance of studying the opposition to racism as this ideology has expressed itself in its major form in this country—namely against African and African-derived peoples. And in the specific examples that will be cited, I shall in this article limit myself to white men and women, knowing full well that the struggle against racism has been a Black-white one and that in it Black people have been the pioneers, the most acute and the most persistent. Still, the facts being what they are, and racism being an affliction of white people in the United States, especially consequential is the history of white opposition to racism. And the fact is that that history is very rich.

The periodization of this anti-racist history would be, I think, as follows: (1) the colonial era; (2) from the Revolutionary era to 1829 and the publication of David Walker's remarkable *Appeal to the Colored Citizens of the World;* (3) 1830 through the Civil War; (4) the Reconstruction era; (5) from about 1890 and Populism to about 1910 and the appearance of the NAACP; (6) from 1910 to the beginning of World War II, with the 1930s marking a transition period, into (7) the era since World War II, marked in particular with the decline of colonialism and of imperialism, the rise of national liberation movements and successes and the spread of socialism into a world-wide system.

One must observe that racism constitutes an element of the more general elitist philosophy which has dominated all class-divided societies in history. One finds this in the views of the aristocracy and nobility concerning the peasantry and so-called common people, in the views of men toward women, in the views of dominant nationalities towards those held in subjection—as English-Irish or German-Polish, etc.

Racism is a form of this class-derived elitism; it is an especially vicious and pernicious form reflecting the fact that the exploitation and oppression of its objects have been especially severe.

This pervasive elitism is reflected in the very language one uses. For example, consider the dual meanings of *poor*—i.e., without money and without merit; or of *rich*—i.e., with money and with merit. Or consider such words as *proper* and then *property* and *propriety* and *proprietor,* and so on. One would require, indeed, a volume to trace this ruling-class impact upon language, past and present and its persistence and weight given the facts that we live in a monopolistic and imperialist—and racist—society.

In Shakespeare's day *wretch* meant peasant; we know what it connotes today. And what it connotes today was really present in the word centuries ago; that is, the peasant *was* a wretch because he was poor; literally, in Calvinistic terms, damned.

If one reads the language with which, for instance, Luther excoriated the rebellious peasants of his time and place and then reads the words of the *Richmond Enquirer* denouncing the rebels who defied death with Nat Turner in Virginia in 1831, or the words with which Ronald Reagan denounced the insurrectionists of Watts in our own day, he will see that not only the content is the same but even the very words are quite identical.

Let the reader consider these examples: here is a French aristocrat's observations in 1689 (La Bruyere):

> Throughout the countryside, one sees wild male and female animals. Black, livid, and all burned by the sun, they are attached to the ground in which they obstinately burrow and dig. They make a noise like speech. When they rise to their feet they show a human face, and, sure enough, they are men. At night, they withdraw into lairs where they live on black bread, water and roots.

And, in Rome, about 195 B.C., Marcus Porcius Cato, tells us:

> Woman is a violent and uncontrolled animal, and it is useless to let go the

reins and then expect her not to kick over the traces. You must keep her on a tight rein . . . Women want total freedom or rather—to call things by their names, total license. If you allow them to achieve complete equality with men, do you think they will be easier to live with? Not at all. Once they have achieved equality, they will be your masters.

In an essay published by UNESCO in 1956, the late Professor Arnold M. Rose offered the opinion that racial prejudice began in the United States at the close of the eighteenth century; indeed, he dated it with extraordinary precision as the Spring of 1793, connecting it, apparently, with Whitney's cotton gin. This, however, forgets the rice, sugar, indigo, tobacco—and cotton—that Black slaves had by then produced for a century within the present boundaries of the United States, let alone the West Indies!

More recently, Professor George M. Frederickson, in a book published in 1971, offers this opinion: "Although societal racism—the treatment of blacks as if they were inherently inferior for reasons of race—dates from the late 17th and 18th century, a rationalized racist ideology did not develop until the 19th century."

These views are erroneous, I think. While the sophistication and pervasiveness of racism was greater in the nineteenth than in the seventeenth and eighteenth centuries, in the earlier period this ideology was part of the superstructure of a slave-based social order and that superstructure derived from, reflected and simultaneously bulwarked that order. Indeed, the remarkable Abbe Gregoire had written as early as December 1789 of racism: "I swear that I am a bit ashamed to fight such an objection [to an egalitarian society] at the end of the eighteenth century!"

This weariness with the fight against racist ideology could be expressed by 1789, since arguments countering racism had been published, for example, by Sir Thomas Browne in 1646, by Richard Baxter in 1673, by Thomas Tryon in 1684; they are in the Germantown Protest of 1688, and in the published writings of William Edmundson (1690), George Keith (1693) and Robert Pyle (1698). With the eighteenth century, confining ourselves to the period prior to the beginning of the American Revolution, something approaching a flood of anti-racist literature appeared. Their authors and relevant dates of their published anti-racist writings are: John Hepburn (1713); John Wise (1717); William Burling (1718); Ralph Sandiford (1729—published, anonymously, by Benjamin Franklin); Elihu Coleman (1733); Benjamin Lay (1737—

published again anonymously, by Benjamin Franklin); John Woolman (1747); Anthony Benezet (1762); James Otis (1764); Benjamin Rush (1773).

To give one a taste of the argumentation, here is Anthony Benezet, writing from significant personal experience, in 1762. He affirmed that he had found "amongst the Negroes as great a variety of talents as amongst a like number of whites; and I am bold to assert, that the notion entertained by some, that the blacks are inferior in the capacities, is a vulgar prejudice, founded on pride and ignorance of their lordly masters, who have kept the slaves at such a distance, as to be unable to form a right judgment of them."

Here in this literature of the pre-Revolutionary period one finds every component of the racist argument systematically combatted. One has, then, in this anti-racist argument the following: (1) a denial of Biblical arguments—such as the so-called curse of Ham—and an insistence upon the equalitarian essence of both Testaments; (2) a denial of bestiality and an insistence upon the humanity of the African and African-derived people and an affirmation that they had souls and the further argument that, therefore, racism was blasphemous; (3) insistence upon specific denials of details of the racist exposition—these almost always coming from those white people with prolonged personal and significant experience and insisting that Black people had the same feelings as other human beings, that they felt remorse, loved children, loved each other, resented injury, rebelled, dreamed of a better life, were able to learn—and the literature often adds—able to learn as well as any other people; (4) an argument pointing to the fact that Black people had among them outstanding individuals, even as other people had and here would appear such names as Dr. James Derham, The Rev. Lemuel Haynes, Benjamin Banneker, John Chavis, Lunsford Lane, Phillis Wheatley, Tom Fuller, etc., depending upon the period of publication; (5) in general, the literature took an environmentalist approach, insisting that where inadequacies appeared they could be reasonably explained in terms of opportunities, conditions, tasks and expectations before Black people.

As racism may be viewed as a form of elitism, so anti-racism was an aspect of the struggle against elitism and in the eighteenth century this meant that anti-racism was an aspect of the movement against feudalism, absolute monarchy, and oppressive colonialism. It was, too, part of a mounting rational, scientific and anti-medieval thought-pattern....

Beyond argumentation and writing, anti-racism manifested itself in activity and in conduct. For example, in 1741 in Charleston, South Carolina, the sympathies of at least three white men were so largely on the side of the slaves—and slave rebels—that they suffered persecution; these were Jonathan Brian, William Gilbert, and Robert Ogle. In 1804 one Jabez Brown, Jr., was driven out of Georgia because of his defense of Black people and his ardent attacks upon slavery. In 1812 a white teacher named Joseph Wood was hanged in New Orleans for suspicion of participating in anti-slavery activities with Black people; and in 1816 George Boxley of Virginia was sentenced to hang for the same "crime" and would have been executed had he not escaped from prison with the aid of his wife. Jailed for defending the right of slaves to rebel, in Charleston in 1822, were four white working men: Andrew Rhodes, William Allen, Jacob Danders and John Igneshias. In 1829 a white printer was forced to flee Georgia because he had been distributing Walker's pamphlet and a white seaman in South Carolina suffered the same fate the same year for the same act.

In terms of conduct one has the realities of the family that raised Benjamin Banneker in Maryland in the early eighteenth century; one has the published work of the late Black scholar, James Hugo Johnston, showing for a limited period in slave Virginia alone twenty-two suits for divorce brought by white men against their wives because of the long-term and close relationship of the women with Black men; or the fact that in that state at that time, of sixty cases of slaves executed on the charge of raping white women, justices recommended mercy in twenty-seven cases because *white people* had presented petitions numerously signed affirming that the white women and the Black men had had voluntary relationships and that no rape had occurred.

Mr. Johnston also revealed that the census manuscript records in one county—where the census taker was more "zealous" than others—showed that nine of the free Black men were living with white wives in 1830. He showed also, that in 1844 local records enumerating Black children in Southampton County noted that nine of them were then living with their white mothers. It can now be added that Peter H. Wood has made similar findings for colonial South Carolina in his work, *Black Majority* (1974). In the center of Virginia, in the town of Staunton, in 1753, the village blacksmith—a very important person, indeed, in the eighteenth century—was a free Black man who had migrated from Lancaster, Pa., with a white wife. Here, then, in Virginia, in the middle of the eighteenth century, lived a Black man and his white wife and he served that community as its most important artisan.

I have confined myself to some notes for the pre-Revolutionary period. One should at least observe that the Abolitionist movement of the nineteenth century had three objectives, not one, and that these were made explicit in the constitutions of the various anti-slavery societies. Those objectives were: (1) the end of slavery; (2) the improvement of the socio-economic conditions of the free Black population; and (3) the elimination of racism and racist practices throughout the United States.

That last objective is neglected in the literature; but it certainly was not neglected by the Abolitionists. A part of the history of anti-racism would be a history of the struggle against jim crow in the United States; that too, has not yet been written.

Remembering the necessary limitations of a magazine article, I shall close at this point. Perhaps enough has been stated to make the point that anti-racism has existed in the United States, that it has had a significant history and that the absence of a literature reflecting that fact is a glaring omission in historiography and a costly lack in the ongoing struggle to cleanse the United States' social order of its single most awful feature.

Published in *The Black Scholar,* VI, January/February 1975, pp. 16-22.

5
HISTORY AND PARTISANSHIP

Falsification in History

Education—literally, the act of leading forward or out—has functioned alas, as an institution seeking to restrain rather than propel and to obscure rather than illuminate.

Books, teachers, administrators, philosophy making up so-called education have reflected and bulwarked class-exploitative systems; hence all have been basically elitist. Given the historic characteristics of class rule—propertied, male supremacist, colonial—education and the control of education hitherto have been largely confined to the male, propertied overlord. In eras preceding the rise of capitalism and its systematic usurpation of the globe, these characteristics have prevailed, in varying forms and degrees, in all civilizations, including African, Asian and pre-Columbian Western Hemisphere. With, however, this usurpation—especially in its monopolist stage—racism appeared as a particularly virulent form of elitism and provided still another variety of false education.

Basic to education and to all education systems—indeed, to any society—is history. The present is made up of the past, and the future is the past and present dialectically intertwined. Controlling the past is of great consequence in determining the present and shaping the future; hence, hitherto exploitative ruling classes have gone to great pains to control that past—that is, to write and teach so-called history.

Historiography has reflected its function and it has bulwarked the class creating it. It has therefore been elitist. . . .

Du Bois, in his preface to my *Documentary History of the Negro People in the United States,* wrote: "We have the record of kings and gentlemen ad nauseam and in stupid detail; but of the common run of human beings, and particularly of the half or wholly submerged working group, the world has saved all too little of authentic record and tried to forget or ignore the little saved."

"Who built the seven towers of Thebes?" Brecht asked. "The books," he replied, "are filled with names of kings."

The history books have been written by the kings' servants for their edification, glorification and sanctification.

In an economy dominated by the bourgeoisie, its scribes dominate the writing of the country's history. The historians whose writings form the core of this nation's textbooks, whose opinions have been soaked up day after day and decade after decade by every literate American, have been from and for the bourgeoisie.

Of one of them—among Bryn Mawr's most distinguished former faculty—Woodrow Wilson, a recent biographer remarked: "He had never known economic insecurity, or poverty, or dread of the future; never had he any intimate contact with men of the working classes." Thus may they nearly all be characterized—the Adamses, (Henry, Brooks and James Truslow), the Bancrofts, (George and Hubert), Beer, Burgess, Channing, Dunning, Fiske, Hart, Mahan, Morison, McMaster, Beard, Oberholtzer, Osgood, Phillips, Rhodes, Schouler, etc.

As one of them, James Ford Rhodes, himself remarked, they conceived of history-writing as an "aristocratic profession" or "the rich man's pastime." These individuals—whose fathers were well-to-do congregational divines (George Bancroft), or secretaries to such as Henry Clay (Fiske), or who were themselves, extremely wealthy men (George L. Beer in tobacco, Rhodes in iron, Beard in dairy-farming), or ghost writers for presidents (Bancroft for Andrew Johnson, McMaster for McKinley), or intellectuals-in-residence at the White House (as Schlesinger, Jr. for Kennedy and Eric Goldman for Lyndon Johnson), or in-laws to president-makers (Mrs. Rhodes was Mark Hanna's daughter), or Rear-Admirals (Mahan and Morison), or editors of frankly big-business organs (as Oberholtzer of the publication of the Iron and Steel Manufacturers Association), or the scion of Confederate Governors and Senators (as Phillips), or quasi-official scribes for

Rockefeller and Ford (as Nevins)—wrote and taught history in very much the same way as bourgeois judges have traditionally interpreted and administered the law, and for very much the same reasons, except that the historians have been less amenable to mass pressure than have been judges.

Naturally such individuals had "a somewhat careful solicitude for the preservation of wealth," as a sympathetic commentator remarked of Schouler; of course, in their books, the "wage earner and farmer rarely appears," as was said of McMaster. Certainly one like Fiske would detest the Populists and Rhodes thought of workers as "always overbearing and lawless," while to Oberholtzer, labor organizers were veritable demons, guilty of "follies and excesses," who turned "foreign rabble" into "murderous mobs." Clearly, such "wretches"—like the Haymarket Martyrs—were destined for "their not unmerited end on the scaffold."

The works of all the "standard" historians exude ultra-nationalism, an almost naive male supremacy, an assumed elitism and a white chauvinism so vicious that they write of the Afro-American people—on the rare occasions they mention them—as another might write of more or less offensive animals.

In this country said the steel baron, Andrew Carnegie, in 1899: "We accept and welcome, as conditions to which we must accommodate ourselves, great inequality of environment, the concentration of business, industrial and commercial, in the hands of a few, and the law of competition between these, as being not only beneficial, but essential for the future of the race."

As the new century dawned, in 1900 William Lawrence, Bishop of the Episcopal Church in Massachusetts and a member of the Harvard Corporation, insisted, ". . . it is only to the man of morality that wealth comes. . . . Godliness is in league with riches. . . . Material prosperity is helping to make the national character sweeter, more joyous, more unselfish, more Christlike."

Surely if there ever was a sweeter, more joyous, more unselfish and more Christlike country than this one with its war in Southeast Asia, its arms shipments to the monsters today ruling Greece, Brazil, Spain, Portugal, Guatemala and Cambodia, with an Eastland as Chairman of the Senate Judiciary Committee, with Mitchell in charge of what is hilariously called justice, with Agnew a heart-beat away from the White House and with the beating heart in the presidency belonging to

Nixon—the world has not seen its like. There is a sweet, joyous unselfish and Christlike quartet if one ever existed: Eastland-Mitchell-Agnew-Nixon! And that quartet finds professors to write their music, from Henry Strangelove Kissinger to Daniel Benign-Neglect Moynihan!

A nation whose most powerful statesmen are the likes of that quartet will have a dominant morality that determines its First Families of Virginia on the basis of the number of slaves their ancestors owned. A human morality would glory not in slave-masters as ancestors, but slaves.

In any humanistic ethic, how could there be a moment's doubt as to which is "inferior" and which is "superior?" If one understands the filth, parasitism, deceit and exploitative essence of ruling classes hitherto, he will, I think, know that it is not the masses, the workers, the producers—the "wretched of the earth"—who are the so-called inferior. They have been subordinate, but they have been the creators; they have been, as the Bible says, "the salt of the earth."

The dynamic history is humanity's struggle to overcome oppression and end exploitation; that is the meaning of the phrase in *The Communist Manifesto,* that "all history is the history of class struggle."

It would be well to examine briefly at this point the problems of historical objectivity so incessantly raised by historians. The question is a twofold one. It involves in the first place the argument between those who differ as to whether or not an historian can be free of assumptions, prejudices, a certain set of beliefs largely guiding both his selection of data and his use of them. It involves in the second place the more profound question as to whether truth as such, good as such, exist or not.

As to the first question, the argument against so-called impartiality has been stated and restated innumerable times, and is overwhelming, but the conclusion generally drawn therefrom—the impossibility of an historical science—does not follow. Certainly, Harry Elmer Barnes is correct when he declares "that no truly excellent piece of intellectual work can be executed without real interest and firm convictions," and that "the notion that the human intellect can function in any vital form in an emotionless and aimless void" is absurd.

Clearly, the challenge offered by men like Beard and Nevins to be shown one "non-partisan" historical work, one work free of a subjective quality, in the sense in which this term is used by them, has not been and apparently cannot be successfully met. The very fact that a human being is the historian—or the natural scientist, for that matter—guarantees the presence of personality, viewpoint, interpretation, selection—in a word, his or her work.

It is then, unquestionably true—indeed, self-evident--as men like Turner and Beard have written, that, to quote the latter, "any written history inevitably reflects the thought of the author in his time and cultural setting." When one says this he demonstrates the inseparability of the past and the present, *but he does not refute the reality of the present*. Carl Becker, anticipating Beard, exclaimed, "O History, how many truths have been committed in thy name." He insisted that the past was a "screen upon which each generation projects its vision of the future." And Harold Temperley felt that when one showed the impossibility of an impartial history he had simultaneously banished the possibility of a science of history. He accepted this "resolution" with vigor and insisted that, therefore, the notion of objectivity was not even "desirable."

Unless one lifts himself above intensely partisan "non-partisanship," unless one sees that though there have been "many truths," there yet may be truth, unless one disengages himself from an ethic premised upon man's exploitation of man, this question of subjectivity is indeed insoluble and one can either ignore it or accept it, but he cannot overcome it.

John Somerville has put this point extremely well:

> The historical materialist believes in absolute right in the same way as he believes in absolute truth, as an objectively existing state of affairs to which our accumulating knowledge and practice become a fuller and fuller approximation, relative because there is something for them to be relative to. Belief in an absolute right [or truth, one may add] is evidently not the same thing as a belief that our knowledge of it is absolutely correct.

This, too, is an essential thesis of Lenin's *Materialism and Empirio-Criticism,* this concept of truth as absolute and knowledge as relative, this conviction that there is an objective yet dynamic reality to which knowledge, as it becomes more and more complete, more and more fully approaches.

Aligning oneself with the rising class, the class whose victory at any given epoch results in enhancing the productive capacities of humanity and invigorating humanistic capacities and thus in making possible the enrichment of life for more and more people, resolves not only the problem of what is good, it resolves the related one of what is true. Only by this complete renunciation of the accepted values and premises of the bourgeoisie may one resolve that class's problem of an infinitely regressive relativism, may one break the bonds of its subjectivity and create, in this sense, an objective history.

Only by the fullest and most complete devotion to one's nation may one achieve internationalism; only by the fullest and most complete understanding of necessity does one arrive at freedom; and only by the fullest and most complete identification with humanity may one achieve objectivity. Here is the theoretical heart of the identity between working-class partisanship and genuine scholarship.

Such a philosophy carries for its upholders the obligation indicated in Allen Johnson's remark that "the more daring and more promising the hypothesis the greater the obligation to tell the truth, the whole truth and nothing but the truth." In our world the most daring and most promising hypothesis is, I think, dialectical and historical materialism.

From those who use it, then, or attempt to use it, one must expect the most rigid adherence to the canons of science, the most uncompromising and relentless search for data and their meanings. This is preeminently a philosophy of life, and those who use it are affecting life. Thus it was, as Engels wrote, that "Marx thought his best things were still not good enough for the workers . . . regarded it as a crime to offer the workers anything less than the very best."

The Marxist conception of history is, as Engels also declared, "above all a guide to study, not a lever for construction after the manner of Hegelians." It is a powerful searchlight, so powerful that if improperly handled it may blind rather than illuminate. And it must be *used,* it must accompany the searcher, who, light in hand, diligently works at unearthing truth.

In this connection one sees the great significance and challenge in the history of the Afro-American people—of Du Bois' crashing chapter, "The Propaganda of History," which concludes his classical *Black Reconstruction.* For these, being the most oppressed and the most exploited, therefore have been the most lied about. This history must not be diluted, or co-opted, in terms of mere "contributions," or of a "me-too" approach as part of a classless, non-dynamic and mythical melting pot. Rather, it can only be comprehended as the inspiring record of battle for self-hood or for freedom and as a fundamental stimulant and part of all democratic, progressive and revolutionary movements in overall United States history—and, for that matter, world history.

Historically, education has sought stability; its function has been to bulwark the status quo. Given the nature of the status quo and the dynamic quality of life—and therefore of science—such education had to be reactionary and basically irrational. Education must be as dynamic as life if it is to serve life; this is at the root of the revolutionary's challenge to educational systems and at the heart of youth's characteristic discontent with such systems. The more informed is that discontent, the better, but be assured that the existence of that discontent is healthy and is among the most hopeful phenomena upon the contemporary scene.

Ascending social classes are wedded to science. That the decadent ones now grasp at every repudiation of reason and make of intellectual despair a lucrative virtue is indicative of their impending doom. Do not the scriptures tell us that the devil rages, "for he knoweth he hath but a short time?"

This paper was delivered April 19, 1970, at a two-day conference on Black Studies held in Bryn Mawr College, Pa. It was published in *Political Affairs,* XLX, June 1970, pp. 53-59.

The American Historical Profession

On October 19 of this year, no less a newspaper than the *Wall Street Journal* headlined a front-page story, "Radical Historians Get Growing Following." It went on to report the existence of "an increasingly influential group of leftist historians who are challenging traditional notions about the nation's past"; that "the leftwing historians are gaining increasing acceptance, both within and without the profession" and that, furthermore, "radicals are also gaining influence in the traditionally conservative American Historical Association, and they are becoming increasingly common on many campuses."

Not unrelated to this development was the report by Robert Reinhold, in the *New York Times* of July 3, 1971, that a Harris Poll among high-school students found that they regarded history as the "most irrelevant" of twenty-one school subjects, and that undergraduate enrollment in history classes at such schools as Harvard, Yale, Stanford and Amherst had dropped by as much as a third in recent years. William V. Shannon, on the other hand, thinks that the findings reported by Mr. Reinhold reflect a nation in which "time vanquished, we lie exhausted alongside our victim"; that "what we have slain is not time but our sense of ourselves as humans. It is that meaninglessness," he concludes, "which pervades this age of instant gratification and instant results and permanent dissatisfaction." *(New York Times,* July 8, 1971.)

Other views are possible. For example, it is not that "our sense of ourselves as humans" has been slain but rather that those whose humanity has long been denied are affirming it with renewed vigor and power; that these have not found and never did find "gratification" and "results," either of the instant or of the long-maturing kind, and that therefore their dissatisfaction has indeed been "permanent" and hence most profound and bitter.

While Mr. Shannon—who is not a teacher—tends to put the blame for the feeling that history as taught is "irrelevant" upon the students who report that view, Professor David F. Kellums, in a recent book asserts: "The history dialogue in our classroom is devoid of relevance. It has become a seemingly endless nightmare, full of sound and fury, signifying nothing. . . . An associate of mine in the Department of History," Mr. Kellum adds, "remarked that Clio was not only dying, but that she was being done in systematically. . . . He also admitted that he did not know how to revive Clio. . . . My own feeling," Mr. Kellums decided, "is that Clio's case is terminal."[1] Professor Martin Duberman has also expressed a despairing view and has, in effect, denied history's relevance: "Though I have tried to make it otherwise," he writes, "I have found that a 'life in history' has given me very limited information or perspective with which to better understand the central concerns of my own life and my own time." *(Evergreen Review,* April 1968.)

Perhaps we get closer to the heart of the problem when we observe that Professors Landes and Tilly, in their work, *History as Social Science* (Prentice-Hall, New York, 1971, p. 6), prepared as part of the survey of the behavioral and social sciences conducted for the National Academy of Sciences and the Social Sciences Research Council, reported, ". . . it must be admitted that history has been misused as a stick to beat reformers and to block change." Recall, also, that the 1969 Annual Meeting of the Organization of American Historians, having the theme "The State of American History: A General Inquiry" was described in the journal of that organization in these words: "The appraisal of American history that emerged from the meeting was surprisingly coherent. Concentrating upon the quality of future scholarship, it accused the profession primarily of narrowness and thoughtlessness." *(Journal of American History,* December 1969, LVI:637; essay on the Meeting by Richard H. Wiebe.)

I think Landes and Tilly are generally correct in their indictment of the historical profession or establishment and the 1969 accusation is fundamentally sound, but I do not think this is a "misuse" of such profession or establishment. I think, rather, that this is the normal and expected functioning of such a profession within the context of its social order and its role therein.

Back in 1885, the president of the University of Michigan wrote to the president of John Hopkins University:

> In the Chair of History the work may lie and often does lie so close to Ethics, that I should not wish a pessimist or an agnostic or a man disposed to obtrude criticism of Christian views of humanity or of Christian principles. I should not want a man who would not make his historical judgments and interpretations from a Christian standpoint.[2]

Of course, there are varying Christian standpoints; Count Metternich and John Brown were both devout Christians but of the two, there is, I think, little doubt as to which Mr. Angell of Michigan or Mr. Gilman of John Hopkins would have preferred for their History Chairs. I suggest, also, that the preference has not terminated with the year 1885.

Professor John Higham, in a book published last year by Indiana University Press, reports that in the late 1940s and in the 1950s: "Unlike the progressive historian [meaning people like Parrington and Beard] his successor did not feel much at odds with powerful institutions or dominant social groups. He was not even half alienated. Carried along in the general postwar reconciliation between America and its intellectuals, and wanting to identify himself with a community, he usually read the national record for evidence of effective organization and a unifying spirit."[3]

What Mr. Higham calls "the general postwar reconciliation" was the era of the intense Cold War and of McCarthyism; the era of the banning of Arthur Miller and Robin Hood; the jailing of the Hollywood Ten; the indicting and trying of Dr. W. E. B. Du Bois; the execution of the Rosenbergs; Virginia's legal lynching of the Martinsville Seven; the exiling of Paul Robeson; the boycotting of Pete Seeger; the blinding of Henry Winston; the firing of thousands of teachers and professors and the refusal to hire additional thousands on racial and political grounds; the era when Louis M. Hacker discovered that the Robber Barons were really Industrial Statesmen and when Professor Allan Nevins left Columbia University to work for the Ford Motor Company. If, as Mr. Higham entitles his book, this is *Writing American History,* no wonder students find that subject the least relevant of all subjects to which they are exposed!

The most thoroughgoing, the deepest challenge to the prevailing structure, practices and purposes of higher education that has ever occurred in the history of the United States is now in process. It seeks to alter basically that structure and those practices and purposes. The structure hitherto, and now, has been and is oligarchic and racist; the practices have been and are snobbish, conservative and racist; the purposes have been and are to bulwark an imperialist and racist social order.

Significant tensions always existed—with periods of more or less intense manifestations thereof—because the universities and colleges could not help reflecting to a degree the class and white supremacist realities and the struggles against them. In addition, the tension sprang specifically from the ostensible purpose of higher learning—i.e., to further scholarship, to seek reality, to advance science. That purpose is, at its heart, in conflict with the structure, purposes and therefore actual practices of most institutions of higher learning in the United States for most of their histories.

The tension is greatest now because imperialism is sicker than ever and notably so in this country; because developments of a socialist and anti-colonialist nature have challenged the ruling class in the United States not only in political-military-diplomatic senses, but also ideologically; because the numerical and qualitative character of the student body (and faculty) have been transformed; and—part of all the above, but still having an identity and impact of its own—because the anti-racist and national liberation developments have reached unprecedented heights and necessarily carry great impact in the United States.

The present challenge to the dominant system of higher education in the United States will persist; it is no more ephemeral than is the worldwide challenge to the system of the private ownership of the means of production. On the contrary; it is part of that challenge. Most of the thinkers seeking to respond to it have not shown, I believe, comprehension of its character let alone afforded any adequate response. I select for brief commentary one of the best products of one of the eminent figures among such thinkers—that entitled "Between the Spur and the Bridle" and consisting of Professor Julian P. Boyd's address at the 1968 gathering of the Association of American University Presses (published in the Spring 1969 issue of *The Virginia Quarterly Review*).

Professor Boyd is the chief editor of the distinguished series of volumes of the papers of Thomas Jefferson. His essay contains many of the virtues of the third president; gracious writing, much learning, wry wit, a concern lest tyranny grow. As to the latter, it is worth noting that not only did Professor Boyd denounce George Wallace in a speech delivered some months prior to the 1968 elections; he was one of the handful of academicians who damned Joseph McCarthy while that statesman was still formidable.

Alas, however, his essay contains many of the limitations of the third president, too; basically elitist, fundamentally racist, and formalistic in its concept of democracy. These failings were serious when manifested in the eighteenth century; today they are positively vitiating.

Professor Boyd's estimate of the U. S. social order and its present government and that government's role in world affairs is positive; his description of the present realities of higher education in the United States is absolutely glowing. In both, he is, I think, wrong and the challengers to such estimates are right.

In a rather unfair passage, Professor Boyd writes that "our self-anointed messiahs" report our society to be corrupt and that the United States "as a nation [is] sick." This is unfair because such findings are reported by people like the chairman of the Senate Foreign Relations Committee and the managing editor of the *New York Times;* Robert Welch might consider J. William Fulbright and James Reston as "self-anointed messiahs," but this seems hardly appropriate for Julian P. Boyd.

The harshness of tone and the *ad hominem* approach reflect perhaps Mr. Boyd's passionate disagreement with those who do not hold with him when he writes that "mistaken as many of the policies [of the U. S.] resulting from our sense of world mission may have been," "yet no great nation in history has exercised its might with comparable restraint and generosity." The inhabitants of Hiroshima and Nagasaki, of North Korea, of Indochina, of Latin America surely would not agree—and the consensus among U. S. college youth today also is otherwise. Many among them see a policy which has been unrestrained and aggressive and they think this policy does not stem from a sense of world mission but rather from a hunger for world hegemony—a *Pax Americana* on the part of the class dominating that nation. They detest the policy and do not experience the hunger and certainly do not wish to satisfy it with their own lives.

Mr. Boyd writes that among the community of intellectuals there have developed qualities permitting "rational discussion" and he names these qualities as "tolerance, generosity, moral courage, justice, decency, and respect for reason." But the consensus, I think, among college youth is that rational discussion has not characterized institutions of higher learning in the United States and that the admirable qualities listed by Mr. Boyd have not permeated its administrative and decision-making and curriculum-making bodies. On the contrary, these have been characterized by timidity, opportunism, arrogance, prejudice, elitism and racism.

Mr. Boyd reports that "our universities and other institutions [have been] designed to give reason a chance"; but these institutions of higher learning have not been so designed. They have been exclusionary; they have been bastions of the status quo; they have been permeated by ugly class, religious and—above all—racial prejudice. And they have permitted themselves to become servitors of the rich and bulwarks of the military-industrial complex. They have trained policemen for fascistic Greece and monarchial Iran and sadistic Saigon puppets; they have masterminded counterrevolutionary strategies in Latin America and the Mid-East; they have served as CIA conduits in Africa, Asia and Eastern Europe; they have justified and rationalized and supported a genocidal war in Indochina which has very nearly destroyed the soul of this Republic.

Their Boards of Trustees are not—as Mr. Boyd chooses to describe them—"the most innocent and least powerful of witches." They are not witches at all; would that they were merely conjured up figures of fevered brains. They are, in fact—and excellent substantiating studies have been published on this—the Hearsts and Rockefellers and Du Ponts and Fords and Gianninis; and the present college generation knows that (even if Mr. Boyd does not). Such people are far from innocent and far from powerless; they do not waste their time on boards and they do hold in their hands the ultimate and the decisive policy-making control over higher education in the United States.

Mr. Boyd ascribes to the seventeenth-century concepts of Locke and the eighteenth-century concept of Madison, a determination to abide by "the will of the majority." But everyone who was anyone in those centuries—reading Locke and Madison—knew that when they spoke of majority they meant majority of those possessing property and that the security of property was—as Locke quite explicitly stated—*the* purpose of government (and further they meant a majority not only of those possessing property but also of those who were male and white). Much of the present student generation in the United States has discovered these secrets—even if the editor of Jefferson has not!

Mr. Boyd fears that the present protesters and dissenters have as their aim "destroying universities and defeating the purposes for which they stand." I do not think these two purposes are synonymous. The purposes which most universities in the United States have furthered most of the time have not been worthy purposes: they are purposes which contradict what should be the purposes of scholarship and of education. Such centers should be *radical;* they should be centers to get at the root of the sickness that does characterize U. S. society. They should be communities of real students and scholars—that is, men and women devoted to making this land one that is free of racism, of poverty, of indignity, of violence and war and to seeking how best to apply all the finest that humanity has hitherto created and how to further develop such creations.

I do not think that Thomas Jefferson—were he alive today—would object to this; at any rate, I believe that this is what the restless student youth and the restless faculty in the United States, Black and white, want. On the success of such an effort depends not the destruction of universities in the United States but their salvation through their transformation meriting the title of institutions of higher learning.

Another recent paper appropriate to our subject moves me to some brief comment. Oscar Handlin of Harvard delivered an address entitled

"History: A Discipline in Crisis?" before the December 1970 Meeting of the American Historical Association (published in *The American Scholar*, Summer 1971). Mr. Handlin states that for some ten years prior to the delivery of that paper he had ceased attending the meetings of the Association; having attended that of 1970, "partly out of nostalgia and partly in response to an invitation suggesting the retrospection appropriate to advancing age," he has come to the conclusion that he "need not soon return."

The meetings of the 1930s and 1940s and 1950s were splendid, Mr. Handlin reports. They conveyed, he says, a sense of "the continuity and integrity of the historical enterprise" and they represented a community of dedicated scholars "inching the world toward truth." Now, he sees the historical profession afflicted with "decay from within"; one of its central difficulties, he writes, is that historians "stagger beneath a burden . . . of making ourselves useful in the solution of society's everchanging problems."

It is likely that Mr. Handlin and I are of the same or very nearly the same age; he writes that the first AHA meeting he attended was that of 1936 and that happens to have been my first meeting too. Of course, what one sees depends largely upon one's angle of vision, and memories are highly personal. Still, as an historian, Mr. Handlin might be interested in another viewpoint and different memories.

The dominant historical profession of the 1930s through the 1950s—as represented in the American Historical Association and what is now called the Organization of American Historians—was a closed, intensely conservative, lily-white, anti-Semitic bulwark and reflection of the same kind of ruling class. When in the 1930s a handful of mavericks called attention to the fact that only white people (and almost always only white men) delivered papers or held offices or conducted key journals or held professorships, we were treated as pariahs. At the most recent meeting of the Organization of American Historians, held in New Orleans, Professor Harrington—lately a president of the University of Wisconsin—mentioned in quite an off-handed way that thirty or twenty years ago there was a general policy in the profession to bar Jews from professorships and, in any case and in any position, to keep their numbers down to a minimum. This was notorious at the time and denounced—by a handful—*at the time.*

In the late 1930s when some daring soul who was a member of the program committee of the AHA actually suggested that perhaps the

Afro-American scholars, Carter G. Woodson or Charles H. Wesley (both holders of doctorates in history from Harvard and authors of distinguished books), might be asked to deliver papers, that hero was removed from the program committee! The most distinguished and creative historian then living in the United States, Dr. W. E. B. Du Bois, was never asked by what is now called the Organization of American Historians and rarely by the American Historical Association to participate in meetings; his masterful and epoch-making work, *Black Reconstruction,* published in 1935, was not reviewed in the *American Historical Review*— and to this day never has been reviewed there! When the Doctor died in the summer of 1963, the *Review* was able to spare one line simply giving the place and date of his demise.

When in the 1930s and 1940s there were shameful witchhunts and people were fired or never hired in various history faculties, there was not a whisper of protest from the community of scholars that Mr. Handlin so lovingly describes. When the witchhunts of the McCarthy era again shamed this nation, all the American Historical Association did was to give that despicable demagogue and his committee the names of "radicals" and to affirm to him and it that the Association deeply regretted their membership. When the dean of American scholarship— Dr. W. E. B. Du Bois, then in his eighties—was arrested and mugged and fingerprinted and tried—for being "an unregistered foreign agent"!—neither Mr. Handlin nor his community of scholars said a mumbling word; they did not even hold their noses in the midst of the stench that poured over this Republic. No, they went on with their meetings and their careers and Mr. Handlin wrote no papers for *The American Scholar* on a profession in crisis.

Of course, times are changing and it is more than just a profession that is in crisis; it is a social order that is in crisis and the profession that hitherto served to bulwark that order deeply feels the crisis.

Now, the college population is not numbered at less than two million with perhaps 40,000 Black students among them as was true before World War II; no, now the college population numbers well over seven million, with 500,000 Black students among them and with a very much larger percentage of young men and women of working-class origins than was true twenty or thirty years ago. That quantitative revolution has helped produce the qualitative change and helps guarantee its continuity.

Today it is not only damned Reds and militant Blacks and enraged women and radical professors (and Angela Davis combines all these virtues) who are hounded and framed, but white Roman Catholic priests and nuns and M.I.T. professors.

No area of intellectual pursuit is more sensitive than that of history; lies about the past feed failures of the present and fuel disasters for the future. Today many of the faculty members who are in their late twenties and early thirties are the products of the post-McCarthy era; they are part of the sit-in and Free Speech and teach-in and Little Rock and Birmingham generation.

They loathed Batista and hailed Castro; they despised Eastland and admired King; they were appalled by the Bay of Pigs and enthralled at the remarkable heroism of the Vietnamese. They may not know what dialectical materialism is; they remain deeply infected by remnants of anti-communism; Scottsboro, Lidice, Stalingrad mean little or nothing to them. But they know—in very large numbers, they know—as between J. Edgar Hoover and Angela Y. Davis who is right and who is wrong and they know which of the two in this society is the chief policeman and which is "America's Most Wanted Criminal."

Many of these now are not only beginning to teach but also beginning to publish; and these—who made heroes of Castro, of Du Bois, of Ho and of Angela—ask not about labels but rather about deeds, about whose side are you on and who are your enemies. They insist on making themselves, to quote Mr. Handlin again, "useful in the solution of society's everchanging problems." They have not lost the hope that once moved Professor Duberman and they have not decided that this aim is incompatible with scholarship. On the contrary, they have decided, rightly, I think, that that is the meaning and purpose of scholarship—that partisanship on the side of the oppressed and exploited is the way to overcome the apparent dilemma of objectivity. That to the degree one identifies with the oppressed, to that degree he has identified with the forces of justice, and that such identity is the way towards objectivity.

Hence, the most creative of these younger practitioners of history have consciously rejected elitism and racism and are producing immensely creative and stimulating works in areas ranging from the Revolutionary period to re-examination of the Cold War era; from the nature of the U. S. Constitution to the nature of the I.W.W.; from realities concerning the KKK to fresh examination of class divisions and extremes of wealth, and social mobility in the United States. And not all the truly radical and piercing work is in U. S. history (I use that in its broadest sense and include therein the particular role of Afro-American and Spanish-speaking and so-called Indian peoples) but there also are American scholars of ancient Rome, of seventeenth and eighteenth-century England and France, and of twentieth-century Britain and Spain as well as of that vast majority of mankind that has never lived in either Europe or in North America.

From great responsibilities flow great opportunities. Faced with the challenge of mastering the past—and rethinking what historians should consider as being "the past"—comprehending the present and thus being better equipped to assist in forging a positive future—what greater opportunity for service exists?

This paper was delivered at the opening of the Sixth Annual Northern Great Plains History Conference; it was attended by 750 historians meeting at Moorehead State College in Minnesota in November 1971. Published in *Political Affairs,* LI, January 1972, pp. 45-54.

NOTES

1. FOUNDING THE REPUBLIC

The Revolutionary Character of the American Revolution

1. V.I.Lenin, "Letter to American Workers," *Lenin on the United States,* New York: International Publishers, 1970, p. 334.
2. Of John Locke (1632-1704), English philosopher and educator, Karl Marx said: " . . . a classical spokesman of the judicial ideas of bourgeois society as distinct from the feudal."

The Declaration of Independence

1. Quoted by Joseph Starobin, *Eye-Witness in Indo-China* (New York, 1954), p. 116.
2. V.I. Lenin, *Collected Works,* Vol. 19 (New York, 1942), p. 48. This was written in March, 1916. [In the most recent edition of Lenin's *Collected Works* this passage, in slightly different translation, may be found in Vol. 22 (Moscow, 1964), p. 144.] - Editor
3. Jared Sparks, *Life of Gouverneur Morris,* Vol. 1 (Boston, 1834), p. 25.
4. Letter dated November 18, 1774, quoted by C.P. Nettels in *George Washington and American Independence* (Boston, 1951), p. 24.
5. Paul Leicester Ford, ed. *The Works of Thomas Jefferson,* Vol. 5 (New York, 1904), p. 189.
6. Quoted by J.H. Hazelton, *The Declaration of Independence,* (New York, 1906), p. 234.
7. C.P. Nettels, *George Washington,* pp. 16, 26.
8. Christopher Ward, *The War of the Revolution,* Vol. 1 (New York, 1952), p. 389. Italics added.
9. Paul Ford, ed. *Works of Jefferson,* Vol. 12, pp. 369-370.
10. Quoted by Julian P. Boyd in his outstanding paper, "Thomas Jefferson and the Police State," *The North Carolina Historical Review,* XXV (April, 1948), p. 247.
11. In his last letter, dated June 24, 1826, in Paul Ford, ed., *Works of Jefferson,* Vol. 12, p. 477.
12. Ralph B. Perry, *Puritanism and Democracy* (New York, 1944), p. 448.
13. Letter dated October 28, 1785, in Paul Ford, ed., *Works of Jefferson,* Vol. 19, pp. 17-18. In this Jefferson is far advanced over Locke or Adam Smith. See on this, Charles M. Wiltse, *The Jefferson Tradition in American Democracy* (Chapel Hill, 1935), pp. 136-139.
14. Frederick Engels, *Anti-Duhring* (New York, 1939) p. 117.

2. PRELUDE TO CIVIL WAR

The Labor Movement in the South During Slavery

1. See: H. Biel, "Class Conflicts in the South, 1850-1860," in *The Communist* (New York), February and March, 1939; R. W. Shugg, *Origins of Class Struggle in Louisiana* (Baton Rouge, 1939); H. Aptheker, *American Negro Slave Revolts* (New York, 1943); and sources cited in those works.
2. K. Marx, *Capital* (International, 1947), I, p. 287.
3. W. H. Russell, *Pictures of Southern Life* (New York, 1861), p. 87.
4. *History of Wages in the U.S. from Colonial Times to 1928*, Bulletin 604, Bureau of Labor Statistics (Washington, 1934), p. 56.
5. *Eighth Census of the United States* (1860), *Manufactures*, p. 725.
6. George R. Taylor, *The Transportation Revolution, 1815-1860* (New York, 1951), p. 79.
7. Though very common, it is incorrect to treat these Southern cities as nothing more than appendages of the plantation system, as does, for example, Louis M. Hacker in *The Triumph of American Capitalism* (New York, 1949, p. 291).Thus, as an instance, only two Southern cities—Savannah, Ga., and Newport, Ky.—gave Breckinridge, slavocracy's presidential candidate, over half their vote in 1860. See the essay by A. Crenshaw in E. F. Goldman, ed., *Historiography and Urbanization* (Baltimore, 1941), pp. 44-66.
8. H. Aptheker, *American Negro Slave Revolts*, and *To Be Free* (New York, 1948), pp. 11-135.
9. R. B. Morris, *Government and Labor in Early America* (New York, 1946), pp. 167-88.
10. Several Southern states, due to such pressure, illegalized the use of slaves in specified occupations, but the laws were never really enforced.
11. Morris, work cited, p. 185.
12. Works Progress Administration, *South Carolina* (New York, 1941), p. 74.
13. Yates Snowden, *Notes on Labor Organization in South Carolina, 1742-1861* (Bulletin of the University of South Carolina, 1914), pp. 10-11; G. G. Johnson, *Ante-Bellum North Carolina* (Chapel Hill, 1937) p. 174; E. A. Wyatt, "Rise of Industry in Ante-Bellum Petersburg" in *William and Mary College Quarterly*, Jan., 1937, p. 20.
14. J. B. McMaster, *A History of the People of the U.S.* (New York, 1903), III, p. 511; Selig Perlman, *A History of Trade Unionism in the U.S.* (New York, 1922), p. 3.
15. McMaster, work cited, III, pp. 511-13; J. R. Commons, and others, eds., *A Documentary History of American Industrial Society* (Cleveland, 1910), III, pp. 245-50; W. P. A., *Maryland* (New York, 1940), p. 78; Perlman, work cited, p. 3.
16. Snowden, work cited, p. 15; W. P. A., *South Carolina*, p. 75; W. P. A., *Louisiana* (New York, 1941), p. 74, Bernard Mayo, *Henry Clay* (Boston 1937), p. 216; A. R. Pearce, "The Rise and Decline of Labor in New Orleans," Master's thesis, (Tulane, 1938).
17. This Charleston paper was one of the earliest advocates of free, public education, "of having all classes, whether rich or poor, educated in Republican national schools." Its "greatest object," it told its worker-readers, was "to urge you to break down the barrier which separates your children from those of lordly aristocrats. . . ." See: *N. Y. Workingmen's Advocate*, Jan. 30, 1830; F. T. Carlton, *Economic Influences Upon Educational Progress in the United States* (Madison, 1908), p. 51; W. P. A., *South Carolina*, p. 75; J. R. Commons, and others, *History of Labor in the U.S.* (New York, 1926), I, p. 286.
18. Snowden, work cited, p. 15; Commons, *Documentary History*, IV, pp. 269-71.

19. W.P.A., *Kentucky* (New York, 1939), p. 67; W.P.A., *South Carolina*, p. 75; R. B. Morris, "Labor Militancy in the Old South" in *Labor and Nation*, May-June, 1948, p. 33; Commons, *History of Labor*, I, pp. 482, 484.

20. J. Kohlemainen, "Reform Activity in Behalf of the Antebellum Needle-women, 1840–1860," in *Social Forces* (1940), XVIII, p. 433; W.P.A., *Maryland* (New York, 1940), p. 78; Commons, *Documentary*, VI, pp. 108–111; J. B. Andrews, "History of Women in Trade Unions," in *Report of Conditions of Women and Child Wage Earners in the U.S.* (Senate Document 645, 61 Cong., 2 sess.), pp. 38–39.

21. R. Nolen, "The Labor Movement in St. Louis prior to the Civil War," in *Missouri Historical Review* (1939), XXXIV, pp. 18–37; W.P.A., *Missouri* (New York, 1941), p. 85; W.P.A., *Louisiana* (New York, 1941), p. 74.

22. Morris, in *Labor and Nation*, IV, p. 33; *Niles' Weekly Register* (Baltimore), June 4, 1836, L, p. 234.

23. W. S. Sanderlin, *The Great National Project: A History of the Chesapeake & Ohio Canal* (Baltimore, 1946), p. 116–22.

24. Morris, in *Labor and Nation*, IV, pp. 32–33.

25. R. Nolen, work cited; W.P.A., *Missouri*, pp. 85–86.

26. *Louisville Examiner*, n.d., in *Anti-Slavery Bugle* (Salem, Ohio), May 4, 1849, cited by Bernard Mandel in *The Negro History Bulletin*, December, 1953.

27. R. Shugg, work cited, pp. 114–16.

28. K. Bruce, "Slave Labor in the Virginia Iron Industry," in *William & Mary College Quarterly* (1926), VI, pp. 295–99; K. Bruce, *Virginia Iron Manufacture in the Slave Era* (New York, 1931), p. 225.

29. C. Lyell, *A Second Visit to the United States* (New York, 1849), II, p. 127; quoted by J. C. Sitterson in *Sugar Country: the Cane Sugar Industry in the South, 1753–1950* (University of Kentucky Press, 1953), p. 61.

30. Shugg, work cited, p. 114; Pearce, work cited; W.P.A., *Louisiana*, p. 74.

31. *Ibid.;* also Commons, *History of Labor*, I, p. 614.

32. Commons, *History of Labor*, II, p. 29; Shugg, work cited, p. 116.

33. R. Shugg, work cited, p. 117.

34. W.P.A., *Kentucky* (New York, 1939), p. 67; W.P.A., *Tennessee* (New York, 1939), p. 84; W.P.A., *Virginia* (New York, 1940), p. 114; H. M. Doughty, "Early Labor Organization in North Carolina, 1880–1900," in *South Atlantic Quarterly* (July, 1935), XXXIV, p. 260.

35. *Southside Democrat*, Jan. 7, 1854, cited by Wyatt, work cited, p. 20.

36. W.P.A., *South Carolina*, p. 75; Broadus Mitchell, *William Gregg* (Chapel Hill, 1928), p. 61. Gregg's workers averaged about $3 per week.

37. J. Grossman, *William Sylvis* (New York, 1945), pp. 26–27, 40, 43.

38. E. A. Wieck, *The American Miners' Association* (New York, 1940), pp. 66–67.

39. *Charleston Daily Courier*, March 26, April 6, 1855, cited by R. B. Morris, in *South Carolina Historical and Genealogical Magazine* (1948), XLIX, p. 195n.; Taylor, work cited, p. 290.

40. J. M. Keating, *History of the City of Memphis* (Syracuse, 1888), I, p. 419; G. M. Capers, Jr., *The Biography of a River Town* (Chapel Hill, 1939), p. 123.

41. Daniel Bell is wrong—not unusual for him—when he writes that from 1850 to 1860 Marxism appeared only "in the large northern cities." (D. Egbert and S. Persons, eds., *Socialism and American Life*, Princeton, 1952, I, p. 231.)

42. Quoted by W. D. Overdyke, *The Know-Nothing Party in the South* 1950), p. 18.

43. Douai came to Philadelphia. That city's Negro community—then the largest in the North—honored him at a public rally, and helped raise funds so that he might publish

a newspaper in Philadelphia. In 1868, Negroes in Texas published a paper using Douai's *Zeitung* press. They sent him a copy of the first number "as a token of gratitude of the colored race that they preserve the memory of his efforts for their freedom."(Morris Hillquit, *History of socialism in the U.S.,* New York, 1903, p. 191; P. S. Foner, *History of the Labor Movement in the U.S.,* New York, 1947, p. 264*n*.)

44. E. W. Dobert, "The Radicals," in A. E. Zucker, ed., *The Forty-Eighters* (New York, 1950), p. 179.
45. Overdyke, work cited, pp. 17–18.
46. H. Montgomery, *Cracker Parties* (Baton Rouge, 1950), p. 127.
47. C. Eaton, *Freedom of Thought in the Old South* (Durham, 1940), p. 228; Overdyke, work cited, p. 17; Zahler, work cited, pp. 102–04.
48. Zahler, work cited, pp. 173–75; Overdyke, work cited, p. 153.
49. The program is published—as an exhibition of horrors—in the speech of an American Party Congressman, W. R. Smith of Alabama, made in the House, Jan. 15, 1855, *Congressional Globe,* 33 Cong., 2 sess., Appendix, p. 95.
50. H. Aptheker, *The Negro in the Civil War* (New York, 1938), pp. 4–8; p. 44; Biel, in *The Communist,* Feb. and March, 1939, and sources therein cited: R. Shugg, work cited; H. Aptheker, *American Negro Slave Revolts.* References to this thesis recur in later writing. A recent example is Bernard Mandel, work cited.
51. Material quoted from Biel, work cited.
52. K. Marx in *Die Presse* (Vienna), November 7, 1861, in K. Marx and F. Engels, *The Civil War in the U.S.* (New York, 1937), p. 79.
53. *Ibid.,* p. 81.
54. For Southern white opposition to the Confederacy, see: A. B. Moore, *Conscription and Conflict in the Confederacy* (New York, 1924); Ella Lonn, *Desertion During the Civil War* (New York, 1928); G. L. Tatum, *Disloyalty in the Confederacy* (Chapel Hill, 1934); J. K. Bettersworth, *Confederate Mississippi* (Baton Rouge, 1941); J. D. Bragg, *Louisiana in the Confederacy* (Baton Rouge, 1941); B. I. Wiley, *The Plain People of the Confederacy* (Baton Rouge, 1943); E. M. Coulter, *The Confederate States of America* (Baton Rouge, 1950); T. C. Bryan, *Confederate Georgia* (Athens, Ga., 1953).
55. Coulter, work cited, pp. 236–37.
56. F. E. Vandiver, *Ploughshares into Swords: Josiah Gorgas and Confederate Ordnance* (Austin, 1952), pp. 165–66, 213–14.
57. R. C. Black III, *The Railroads of the Confederacy* (Chapel Hill, 1952), p. 333.
58. For example, the *Richmond Examiner,* Jan. 30, 1864.
59. William R. Plum, *The Military Telegraph During the Civil War in the U.S.* (Chicago, 1882), II, pp. 116–19.

4. RACISM AND CLASS CONSCIOUSNESS

Class Conflicts in the South: 1850 – 1860

1. G. Johnson, *Ante-Bellum North Carolina* (Chapel Hill, 1937), p. 478; J. Redpath, *The Roving Editor* (New York, 1859), p. 127.
2. J. S. C. Abbott, *South and North* (New York, 1860), p. 124.
3. F. L. Olmsted, *A Journey in the Back Country* (London, 1860), pp. 474–75.
4. *The Liberator* (Boston) January 10, 1851; H. Wright, *The Natick Resolution* (Boston, 1859), passim.
5. Quoted in W. Chambers, *American Slavery and Colour* (London, 1857), pp. 154–55.
6. A. Ross, *Memoirs of a Reformer* (Toronto, 1893); J. Redpath, *The Roving Editor;* A. Abel and F. Klingberg, *A Sidelight on Anglo-American Relations* (New York, 1927), p. 258.

7. W. H. Siebert, *The Underground Railroad* (New York, 1899), pp. 28, 152.
8. *Journal of Southern History* (1935), I., p. 33; See also R. Ogden, *Life and Letters of E. L. Godkin*, Vol. 1 (New York, 1907), pp. 122, 143; F. L. Olmsted, *Back Country*, pp. 62, 82, 446.
9. G. Johnson, *Ante-Bellum North Carolina*, p. 496; F. L. Olmsted, *Journey to the Seaboard Slave States*, Vol. 1, (New York, 1904), p. 32.
10. *Richmond Daily Dispatch*, September 5, 1856, August 24, 1858; J. Stirling, *Letters from Slave States* (London, 1857), p. 295.
11. *Liberator*, January 29, 1858, citing Franklin *Sun*, and July 8, 1859, citing St. Louis *Democrat*. See also *Freeman's Journal* (Philadelphia) August 7, 1852, citing Fredericksburg *Herald*; W. Chambers, *American Slavery*, appendix; H. Trexler, *Slavery in Missouri* (Baltimore, 1914), p. 72.
12. F. L. Olmsted, *Back Country*, pp. 445-46.
13. New York *Weekly Tribune*, September 16, 1854, April 19, 1856, February 7, 1857, citing Montgomery *Journal*.
14. H. T. Catterall, *Judicial Cases Concerning Slavery*, Vol. 3, (Washington, 1932), p. 648.
15. *Louisiana Historical Quarterly* (1924) VII, p. 230, citing *Daily True Delta*; Document No. 46, *House of Delegates*, 1852, Virginia State Library, Richmond.
16. For other examples see *Executive Papers* for December, 1859, and January, November, December, 1860, in archives division, State Library, Richmond; New Orleans *Daily Picayune*, November 25, 30 and December 2, 1856.
17. W. H. Siebert, *Underground Railroad*, p. 26; S. Mitchell, *Horatio Seymour* (Cambridge, 1938), p. 482; F. L. Olmsted, Vol. 2, *Seaboard*, p. 150.
18. W. Hesseltine, *A History of the South* (New York, 1936), p. 258; W. H. Siebert, *Underground Railroad*, p. 44.
19. F. L. Olmsted, *Seaboard*, Vol. 1, p. 182.
20. *Richmond Daily Dispatch*, September 17, 1856; *Annual Report of American Anti-Slavery Society ... for year ending May 1, 1859*, (New York, 1860), p. 84.
21. Citation in detail for these figures would require too much space. They are taken from the *Acts of the General Assembly of Virginia* for each of the years mentioned.
22. The sources used for this are the New Orleans *Daily Picayune*, June 14, 15, 16, 23, 1853; *The Liberator*, June 24, July 1, 8, 1853, citing other Southern newspapers.
23. *Governor's Letter Book* (MS.), No. 43, pp. 514-15, Historical Commission, Raleigh, North Carolina.
24. Austin *State Gazette*, September 27, 1856; F. L. Olmsted, *A Journey Through Texas* (New York, 1860), pp. 503-04, quoting other Texas papers.
25. New York *Weekly Tribune*, November 15, 1856, citing Ouchita, Louisiana, Register; Austin *State Gazette*, November 15, 1856; New Orleans *Daily Picayune*, November 16, 1856.
26. New Orleans *Daily Picayune*, November 27, December 2, 1856.
27. *The Liberator*, November 28, December 12, 1856, citing local papers.
28. Milledgeville *Federal Union* quoted in U. B. Phillips, *Plantation and Frontier*, Vol. 2 (Cleveland, 1909), p. 116.
29. Support for this and the following paragraph will be found in *Letter Books of the Governors of North Carolina* (Ms.) T. Bragg, No. 43, pp. 635, 636, 639, 653, 654, located in Raleigh: New Orleans *Daily Picayune*, December 12, 13, 23, 24, 25, 26, 1856; Richmond *Daily Dispatch*, December 9, 10, 11, 12, 15, 1856; New York *Weekly Tribune*, December 13, 20, 1856, January 3, 1857; *The Liberator*, December 12, 1956; *Annual Report of the American Anti-Slavery Society 1857-1858*, pp. 76-77; J. Stirling, *Letters From Slave States*, pp. 51, 59, 91, 294, 297-98. F. L. Olmsted, *Back Country*, pp. 474-75; *Journal of Southern History*, I. pp. 43-44. An escaped German

revolutionist, Adolph Douai, published an Abolitionist paper in San Antonio, Texas, from 1852 until 1855, when he was driven out. See M. Hillquist, *History of Socialism in the United States* (New York, 1910), p. 171.

30. Copied by Richard H. Coleman in a letter, asking for arms, dated Carolina county, December 25, 1856, to Governor Henry Wise, in *Executive Papers*, archives division, State Library, Richmond. Other letters in this source show that the governor in December 1856, received requests from and sent arms to fifteen counties.

31. Letter from Montgomery County, Tennessee, originally in *The New York Times*, in *The Liberator*, December 19,1856; see also New York *Weekly Tribune*, December 20, 27, 1856, quoting local papers, and *Atlantic Monthly* (1858), II., pp. 732–33.

32. *Principia*, New York, December 17, 1859.

33. Letters quoted are to Governor Letcher from P. Williams, January 5, 1860, and C. C. Larue, January 17, 1860, in *Executive Papers*, State Library, Richmond.

34. *Principia*, New York, January 7, 1860, quoting Missouri *Democrat*. Karl Marx read reports of this revolt. See his comment and Engels' reply in *The Civil War in the United States*, (New York, 1937), p. 221.

35. Austin *State Gazette*, July 14, 28, August 4, 11, 18, 25, 1860; John Townsend, *The Doom of Slavery* (Charleston, 1860), pp. 34–38.

36. *Journal of Southern History*, I. p. 47.

37. *Liberator*, August 24, 1860

38. St Louis *Evening News* quoted in *The Liberator*, October 26, 1860.

39. Material on this is in the *Executive Papers*, November 1860, State Library, Richmond.

40. R. B. Flanders, *Plantation Slavery in Georgia*, (Chapel Hill, 1933), p. 275.

41. New York *Daily Tribune*, January 3, May 29, August 5, 1861.

42. Edmund Kirke (J. R. Gilmore), *Among the Pines* (New York, 1862), pp. 20, 25,59,89,90–91,301.

43. A. C. Cole, *The Irrepressible Conflict* (New York, 1934), p. 34; L. C. Gray, *History of Agriculture in the Southern United States*, Vol. 2 (Washington, 1933), p. 656.

44. W. Hesseltine, *Journal of Negro History*, 1936, XXI, p. 14.

45. See two studies by J. Chandler, *Representation in Virginia* (Baltimore, 1896), pp. 63–69; *History of Suffrage in Virginia* (Baltimore, 1901), pp. 49–54; C. H. Ambler, *American Historical Review*, 1910, XV, pp. 769–76.

46. H. M Wagstaff, *State Rights . . . in North Carolina* (Baltimore, 1906), p. 111.

47. *Memoirs of W. W. Holden* (Durham, 1911), p. 5; C. C. Norton, *The Democratic Party in Ante-Bellum North Carolina*, (Chapel Hill, 1930), p. 173.

48. W. K. Boyd, *Trinity College Historical Society Publications*, Vol. 5 (New York, 1905), p. 31: H. M. Wagstaff, *State Rights*, p. 110; C. C. Norton, *The Democratic Party*, pp. 199–204.

49. *Annual Report of the American Historical Association*, 1910, p. 174.

50. In 1849 a white man was tried for incendiarism in Spartanburg, South Carolina, and one of the pieces of evidence against him was a pamphlet by "Brutus" called *An Address to South Carolinians* urging poor whites to demand more political power. Another pamphlet of similar purport is mentioned as being circulated in South Carolina in 1843. See H. Henry, *Police Control of Slaves in South Carolina* (Emory, 1914), p. 159; D. D. Wallace, *History of South Carolina*, Vol. 3, (New York, 1934), p. 130.

51. Laura A. White in *South Atlantic Quarterly*, 1929, XXVIII, pp. 370–89; Laura A. White, *Robert B. Rhett* (New York, 1931), p. 123 and Chapter VIII; D. D. Wallace, *South Carolina*, Vol. 3, pp. 129–38.

52. For accounts of similar contests elsewhere see, T. Abernethy, *From Frontier to Plantation in Tennessee* (Chapel Hill, 1932), p. 216; C. Ramsdell, *Studies in Southern*

History and Politics (New York, 1914), p. 66; W. E. Smith, *The F. P. Blair Family in Politics*, Vol. 1 (New York, 1933), pp. 292, 300, 337, 400, 416, 440.

53. J. B. Ranck, *Albert G. Brown* (New York, 1937), p. 65.
54. Cole, *The Whig Party in the South* (Washington, 1913), p. 72; it is true that an anti-Negro feeling was often mixed with anti-slavocratic feeling of the poor whites. Nevertheless, the latter feeling *was* present. For example, Hinton R. Helper was anathema to the slavocracy notwithstanding the fact that he was possessed of a vicious anti-Negro prejudice.
55. F. L. Olmsted, *Back Country*, p. 180; Stirling, *Letters*, p. 326; J. Aughey, *The Iron Furnace* (Philadelphia, 1863), pp. 39, 228; see G. G. Johnson, *Ante-Bellum North Carolina*, p. 577.
56. W. S. Jenkins, *Pro-Slavery Thought in the Old South* (Chapel Hill, 1935), p. 240.
57. Following title page of A. Cole's *Irrepressible Conflict*.
58. See, *The Liberator*, February 1, 1856; R. Taylor, *North Carolina Historical Review*, 1925, II, p. 331.
59. Charlotte, North Carolina, *Western Democrat*, June 12, 1860.
60. Senator A. G. Brown of Mississippi quoted by Ranck, *Albert G. Brown*, p. 147; see also W. Bean in *North Carolina Historical Review*, 1935, XIII, p. 115.
61. Olmsted, *Seaboard*, II, pp. 149–50, quoting a South Carolina paper.
62. Mobile, *Mercury*, quoted in New York *Daily Tribune*, January 8, 1861.
63. J. S. Abbott, *South and North* (New York, 1860), p. 150.
64. G. G. Johnson, *Ante-Bellum North Carolina*, p. 78.
65. *DeBow's Review*, January 1850, quoted by P. Tower, *Slavery Unmasked*, (Rochester, 1856), p. 348, emphasis in original.
66. Charleston *Mercury*, February 13, 1861, in *Political Science Quarterly*, 1907, XXII, p. 428; see D. Dumond, *The Secession Movement* (New York, 1931), p. 117.
67. H. M. Wagstaff, *State Rights*, p. 145.
68. D. D. Wallace, *History of South Carolina*, Vol. 2, p. 130.
69. L. A. White, *Rhett*, p. 177; see also Marx to Engels, July 5, 1861, in their *Civil War in the United States*, pp. 228–30, where the votes in the secession conventions are analyzed.
70. C. C. Norton, work cited, p. 204.
71. L. A. White, *Rhett*, p. 202.

5. HISTORY AND PARTISANSHIP

The American Historical Profession

1. David F. Kellums, *The Socialist Studies: Myths and Realities*, (New York, 1969).
2. Quoted in Laurence R. Veysey, *The Emergence of the American University*, (Chicago, 1965), p. 75.
3. John Higham, *Writing American History: Essays on Modern Scholarship*, (Bloomington, Indiana, 1970), p. 144.

BIBLIOGRAPHICAL COMMENT

The history of the Afro-American people runs as a central thread through the history of the United States. Without detailed knowledge of it, comprehension of the history of the country as a whole is impossible.

Herbert Aptheker commenced his scholarly activities in the mid-nineteen thirties. At that time the established view of the Afro-American people among white academics may be summarized by quoting from William E. Woodward's then best-selling biography, *Meet General Grant* (New York: H. Liveright, 1928; and reprinted in 1946). The Negro, Woodward explained, "is lovable as a good-natured child, with a child's craving for affection, but his easy temper is deceptive. It is merely the pliability of surrender, the purring of a wild creature that has been caught and tamed." Woodward continued: "Negroes are the only people in the history of the world, so far as I know, that ever became free without any effort of their own. . . . It [the Civil War] was not their business. They had not started the war nor ended it. They twanged banjos around the railroad stations, sang melodious spirituals and believed that some Yankee would soon come along and give each of them forty acres of land and a mule."

Herbert Aptheker's life work has been a refutation of those assertions. He was virtually alone among white historians when he began. Original sources for such research were largely unknown. And, aside from the pioneering studies of such Black historians as Drs. Carter G. Woodson, Charles H. Wesley and W. E. B. Du Bois, the secondary sources were racist, pro-slavery tracts.

Aptheker believed, as he wrote in the introduction to one of his earliest books, *To Be Free* (1948) that only "prolonged and rigorous research . . . into the still largely untapped source material" would provide for an "overall history worthy" of the Afro-American people. "Nothing can replace this basic procedure in scientific investigation," he continued, "and it is only on the strength of such digging and probing, such sifting and weighing, that the discipline of Negro historical writing will be lifted from the level of fantasy, wish-fulfillment and bigotry, into the realm of fact and reality."

Aptheker's work reflects this meticulous attention to detail. Starting in seventeenth century archives in states along the Eastern seaboard, and the slave states in particular, Aptheker combed through newspapers, journals, diaries, military and naval records, police reports, court cases and congressional and state legislative records, and continued the painstaking reconstruction of Black history begun by Du Bois, Woodson and Wesley. He began assembling and publishing his findings in 1937. Between then and the end of the Second World War, Aptheker completed his master's thesis on Nat Turner, his doctoral dissertation on slave revolts, and additional essays on slavery and the struggle against it, as follows (in chronological order):

Nat Turner's Revolt: the environment, the event, the effects. Unpublished master's thesis, Columbia University, 1937. Published, New York: Humanities Press, 1966; Grove Press, 1968.

"American Negro Slave Revolts," *Science & Society* I (Summer, 1937):512-538; and II (Summer, 1938):386-392.

"Class Conflicts in the South: 1850-1860." *The Communist* XVIII (February & March, 1939):170-181; 274-279, Written under Aptheker's pseudonymn, H. Biel. Later published in *Toward Negro Freedom,* New York: New Century Publishers, 1956; and in the present volume.

A related work, though published later, is *The Labor Movement in the South During Slavery,* New York: International Publishers, 1954. Also published in this volume.

"Maroons Within the Present Limits of the United States." *Journal of Negro History* XXIV (April, 1939):167-184. In slightly revised form Aptheker published this under the title, "Slave Guerilla Warfare" in his book, *To Be Free. Studies in American Negro History.* New York: International Publishers, 1948.

"Negroes Who Served in Our First Navy." *Opportunity* XVIII (April, 1940):117.

"The Quakers and Negro Slavery." *Journal of Negro History* XXV (July, 1940):331-362. This essay, under the same title, appears in Aptheker's *Toward Negro Freedom* (1956).

"They Bought Their Way To Freedom." *Opportunity* XVIII (June, 1940):180-182. Revised and lengthened this appears under the title "Buying Freedom" in *To Be Free* (1948).

"Negro History: A Cause for Optimism." *Opportunity XIX (August,* 1941):228-231.

"Militant Abolitionism." *Journal of Negro History.* XXVI (October, 1941):438-484.

"Negroes in the Abolitionist Movement." *Science & Society* V (Winter, 1941):2-23. This was also published as a pamphlet, *The Negro in the Abolitionist Movement.* New York: International Publishers, 1940. And, it appears as one of the chapters in Aptheker's *Essays in the History of the American Negro.* New York: International Publishers, 1945; 1964.

Between 1938 and 1941 Aptheker produced four pamphlets: *The Negro in the Civil War; Negro Slave Revolts in the United States, 1526-1860; The Negro in the American Revolution;* and *The Negro in the Abolitionist Movement.* These were combined into a book, *Essays in the History of the American Negro* (New York: International Publishers, 1945).

In 1943 Aptheker's dissertation, *American Negro Slave Revolts,* was published by Columbia University Press. To fulfill requirements for the doctorate, Columbia then required publication of the dissertation. In 1952 the copyright was transferred to International Publishers which has since reissued the book on four occasions (1963, 1969, 1974, 1978).

With characteristic acumen, Aptheker observed in his preface to the 1969 edition that: "Writing on slave unrest in the United States—and doing this in 1969—one feels more like a news reporter than a historian. While recently the

California statesman, Ronald Reagan, found the ghetto rebels of today 'mad dogs,' a South Carolina statesman of 1823 found plantation rebels of his day to be 'monsters in human shape.' Which humans are dogs and monsters depends, I suggest, upon class and, often upon color and nationality, too."

Having tunneled so deeply into the archival sources, Aptheker mined a veritable mountain of priceless nuggets in the form of petitions, appeals, pamphlets and letters attesting to the Black quest for freedom. Without benefit of duplicating facilities as we know them today, he copied the documents he found—totalling some two million words—by hand. And, in 1951 Aptheker published the first volume of *A Documentary History of the Negro People in the United States, From Colonial Times to the Founding of the NAACP in 1910.* Volumes II and III were complete in 1973 and 1974 respectively—Volume II covering the period between the founding of the NAACP and the New Deal; and Volume III spanning the FDR years through the end of World War II (New York: Citadel Press, 1951: Secaucus, New Jersey: Citadel Press, 1973 and 1974).

Also after the war, *To Be Free, Studies in American Negro History,* which Aptheker marks as his favorite book, was published (New York: International Publishers, 1948). It included the previously mentioned essays on guerrilla warfare, buying freedom and abolitionism. Hitherto unpublished chapters on aspects of the Civil War and Reconstruction completed the work.

Additional, more recent studies in Afro-American history by Herbert Aptheker, include (in chronological order):

Toward Negro Freedom. Historic Highlights in the Life and Struggles of the American Negro People from Colonial Days to the Present. New York: New Century Publishers, 1956. Especially consequential here is the essay on "America's Racist Laws," originally published under that title in *Masses & Mainstream* IV (July, 1951):40–56.

Soul of the Republic. The Negro Today. New York: Marzani & Munsell, 1964. Outstanding in this book is the tribute to W. E. B. Du Bois, written shortly after his death. This volume also contains a useful analysis of the status and conditions of Black people nationally and in the various states, as prepared by the U.S. government in 1963.

And Why Not Every Man? Documentary Story of the Fight Against Slavery in the U.S. Berlin: Seven Seas Publishers, 1961; and New York: International Publishers, 1970. Often mistaken for being a selection from Aptheker's *Documentary History of the Negro People,* this work is actually an entirely separate effort.

Afro-American History: The Modern Era. Secaucus, New Jersey: Citadel Press, 1971. Focusing on the freedom struggle in the twentieth century, this work contains several significant essays including: "Afro-American Superiority: A Neglected Theme in the Literature," originally published in *Phylon* XXXI (Winter, 1970):336–343; "American Imperialism and White Chauvinism," originally published in *Jewish Life* IV (July, 1950): 21–24; and "The Black College Student in the 1920's—Years of Preparation and Protest."

Two other significant essays by Aptheker in Afro-American history should be indicated: "The Negro Woman," *Masses & Mainstream* II (February, 1949):10–17; and a pamphlet, *Negro History: Its Lessons for Our Time* (New York: New Century Publishers, 1956).

At the height of the McCarthy era when many Communists and progressives were jailed and persecuted, Aptheker commenced a series of articles in the *Daily Worker* detailing the history of political prisoners in the United States. Between June 8 and September 3, 1953, accounts of the trials of political activists in the revolutionary era, during the anti-slavery crusade, in the woman's suffrage movement, in Latin America and the Philippines in the early part of the century as U.S. imperialism advanced its colonial empire, and in the socialist and labor movements of the 1920s and 1930s appeared.

Implicit in all of Aptheker's work, of course, is a polemic against predominant trends in the American historical profession. At times, Aptheker made the argument explicit, and in this regard too, his work is consequential. A major effort was his *Laureates of Imperialism: Big Business Re-Writes American History* (New York: *Masses & Mainstream,* 1954). Useful also is Aptheker's critique of history writing on the American Revolution which introduces his essay, "Was the American Revolution A Majority Movement?" *Political Affairs* XXXV (July, 1956):1–10; and his "Black Studies and U.S. History," *Political Affairs* L (December, 1971):50–57, which is reprinted in his *Afro-American History: The Modern Era* (1971) under the title "Black Studies: Realities and Needs."

Attendant to the recent escalation of racist violence in the United States has been the simultaneous intensification of racist ideology emanating from professional and literary circles. Aptheker's critiques have been prompt and devastating. Some of the more important are listed below (in chronological order):

"Legacy of Slavery: Comments on Eugene D. Genovese." *Studies on the Left* VI (November-December, 1966):27–34. This essay with some additions appeared under the title: "Slavery, the Negro and Militancy," *Political Affairs* XLVI (February, 1967):36–43. At the Socialist Scholars Conference in New York City in the Fall of 1966 Eugene Genovese presented a paper entitled, "The Legacy of Slavery and the Roots of Black Nationalism." This paper together with comments by Aptheker and C. Vann Woodward of Yale University's History Department, appeared in the above cited issue of *Studies on the Left.* Genovese's paper represented the main ideas in his book, *The Political Economy of Slavery; Studies in the Economy & Society of the Slave South.* New York: Pantheon Books, 1965.

"Styron-Turner and Nat Turner: Myth and Truth," *Political Affairs* XLVI (October, 1967):40–50. This was Aptheker's criticism of Styron's novel: *The Confessions of Nat Turner* (New York: Random House, 1967). Subsequently, Aptheker published an addendum to the first review, "Styron's Nat Turner Again." *Political Affairs* XLVII (April, 1968):47–50. Another of Aptheker's reviews appeared in *The New Student South* V (May, 1968):3–7; and in *The Nation* CCVI (April 22, 1968):543–547. The review/essay by Aptheker which appeared in *Political Affairs,* was subsequently published in his *Afro-American History: The Modern Era* (1971).

"Racism & Historiography," *Political Affairs* XLIV (May, 1970):54–57.

"Banfield: The Nixon Model Planner." *Political Affairs* XLIX (December, 1970):34–45. This is a review/essay of the book by Edward Banfield, *The Unheavenly City: The Nature and Future of Our Urban Crisis.* Boston: Little, Brown, 1970.

"Heavenly Days in Dixie: Or, the Time of their Lives." *Political Affairs* LIII (June & July, 1974):40–54; 44–57. This is a review/essay of the book by Robert W. Fogel and Stanley L. Engerman, *Time on the Cross: The Economics of American Negro Slavery.* Boston: Little, Brown, 1974.

"The Struggle Against Racism: Myths and Realities," *Political Affairs*, LVI (April, 1977): 28–34. A review/essay of Nathan Glazer's social-democratic attack on affirmative action in his book titled, *Affirmative Discrimination: Ethnic Inequality and Public Policy*. New York: Basic Books, 1975.

Utilizing his basic focus on Afro-American history as the special vantage point from which to view all of American life, and expanding his research efforts, Aptheker, in the mid-nineteen fifties, commenced writing a twelve-volume Marxist history of the United States, all to be published by International Publishers. Volume I, *The Colonial Era* appeared in 1959; and Volume II, *The American Revolution, 1763-1783* was published in 1960, and Volume III *Early Years of the Republic, From the End of the Revolution to the First Administration of Washington* (1783-1793) came in 1976. Volume IV is now in progress.

At the present time Herbert Aptheker is the editor of the projected forty volume *Collected Published Works of W. E. B. Du Bois*, under the auspices of the Kraus-Thomson Organization Limited, in Millwood, New York. In connection with this project Aptheker produced a 600-page *Annotated Bibliography of the Published Writings of W. E. B. Du Bois* (1973). Aptheker is also the editor of *The Selected Correspondence of W. E. B. Du Bois*, a three-volume series under the auspices of the University of Massachusetts Press. Volume I of the *Correspondence*, with selections from 1877 to 1934 was published in 1973. Volume II (1934-1944) appeared in 1976, and Volume III (1944-1963) in 1978.

BETTINA APTHEKER, JUNE 1978.

NAME INDEX